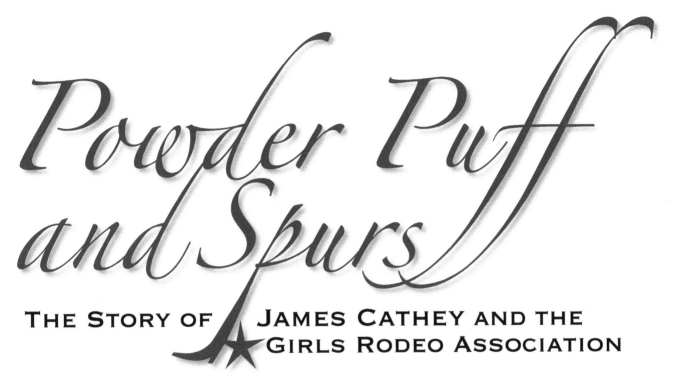

Powder Puff and Spurs

The Story of James Cathey and the Girls Rodeo Association

CRAIG W. CATHEY
AND
GORDON CATHEY

FEATURING HISTORIC PHOTOGRAPHS BY
JAMES CATHEY

Use of Photographs and Other Images

All of the images in this book are protected by U.S. copyright, but most are available to the public for private and commercial use by way of limited license, which must be obtained from the owner of the copyright of each individual image and for each individual use.

Most of the photographs in this book are from the collection of photographic negatives produced by James Cathey, owned by the National Cowboy & Western Heritage Museum, and housed in the museum's Donald C. & Elizabeth M. Dickinson Research Center. Each of these James Cathey images is labeled with "James Cathey photo–2015.006," followed by additional characters. In each case, the complete string of characters can be used to locate the specific image within the overall collection. The copyright of every James Cathey photo is owned by the publisher of this book, James Cathey Heritage Collection, LLC, and the company may enforce restrictions on any specific use of any specific image. Access to the use of one or more of the James Cathey images should begin with a request submitted in writing to:

Director and Curator of Archives
Dickinson Research Center
National Cowboy & Western Heritage Museum,
1700 NE 63rd Street, Oklahoma City, Oklahoma 73111

Other photographs and historic images in this book are labeled as to their sources, and each of them is protected by copyright. For access to any image not labeled as "James Cathey photo..." Please contact the source shown with the image. One source other than the National Cowboy & Western Heritage Museum that was used for multiple images in this book is:

National Cowgirl Museum and Hall of Fame
1720 Gendy Street, Fort Worth, Texas 76107

Published by
James Cathey Heritage Collection, LLC
7311 Wild Valley Drive, Dallas Texas 75231
Email: info@jamescathey.com
Website: jamescathey.com

ISBN 978-0-692-14430-5
Library of Congress Control Number: 2018911341

Printed in the United States of America

DEDICATED TO THE MEMORY OF

JAMES J. CATHEY
AND
MARGIE ELEASE JOHNSON CATHEY

Halls of Fame

Many of the outstanding individuals written about in this book are honored members of one or more Halls of Fame related to their stellar careers in rodeo or other western horse sports. Several of these halls are mentioned in this book with short names. They include the following:

National Cowgirl Hall of Fame, National Cowgirl Museum and Hall of Fame, Fort Worth, Texas

National Cutting Horse Association Hall of Fame, Fort Worth, Texas

ProRodeo Hall of Fame and Museum of the American Cowboy, Colorado Springs, Colorado

Rodeo Hall of Fame, National Cowboy & Western Heritage Museum, Oklahoma City, Oklahoma

Texas Cowboy Hall of Fame, Fort Worth, Texas

Texas Rodeo Hall of Fame, Pecos, Texas

Texas Rodeo Cowboy Hall of Fame, Fort Worth, Texas

CONTENTS

Acknowledgments

We are particularly indebted to the staff of the Donald C. & Elizabeth M. Dickinson Research Center at the National Cowboy & Western Heritage Museum: **Kimberly Roblin,** Director & Curator of Archives; **Karen Spillman,** Librarian; and **Kera Newby** and **Holly Hasenfratz,** Digital & Manuscript Archivists. They not only opened their archives to us, provided space and resources and cheerfully retrieved the materials we needed, but continued to respond quickly to our subsequent queries and requests. **Bethany Dodson,** Research and Education Manager at the National Cowgirl Museum and Hall of Fame, was equally helpful, giving us access to precious archives, space to work, and her patient support of our research efforts. The staff at *Western Horseman* was also very helpful: **Ernie King,** Publisher, **Ross Hecox,** Editor in Chief; **Christine Hamilton,** Editor; **Tonya Ward,** Business Manager; and **Tim Gelnaw,** Warehouse Manager.

In addition, **Megan Winterfeld,** Exhibits and Collections Coordinator at the ProRodeo Hall of Fame and Museum of the American Cowboy, and **Ann Bleiker,** Managing Editor of *WPRA NEWS,* were forthcoming with much needed help.

Special thanks to filmmakers **Steve Wursta** and **Amanda Micheli,** who each went way beyond the call of duty and copied their excellent out-of-print films so that we might augment our research.

For consulting, guidance and editing assistance, we thank Networlding Publishing, Inc.: **Melissa G. Wilson,** President; and **Becky Blanton** and **Gretchen Dykstra.**

We were honored to be able to interview six members of the National Cowgirl Hall of Fame, who created and lived this rodeo history:

- **Mary Ellen "Dude" Barton**
- **Betty Barron Dusek**
- **Dixie Reger Mosley**
- **Jimmie Gibbs Munroe**
- **Rhonda Sedgwick-Stearns**
- **Florence Youree**

We will always treasure our time with these fascinating women. Getting to know them personally was the highlight of our journey during this past year.

Among the many other individuals whose help was invaluable are **Gail Hughbanks Woerner,** rodeo historian and author; **Kathy Crowe Wright,** former professional trick rider; **Ron Williams,** graphic artist; and **Renée M. Laegreid,** author and Professor, History of the American West, University of Wyoming.

We owe our deepest thanks to our extended familiy for their patience and unflagging support. Deserving individual mention are Gordon's spouse, **Patricia A. Cathey;** Craig's spouse, **Barbara Yount Cathey, PhD;** and sister-in-law **Mary Laurie Cathey.**

Craig W. Cathey
Gordon Cathey

With special appreciation for the late

Margaret Clark Formby
Founder of the
National Cowgirl Hall of Fame

without whose vision and dedication
much of the history contained herein might
have been lost forever

FORWARD

By Gail Hughbanks Woerner

There's nothing more rewarding than working at something you love. Having a passion for how you make your living can be one of the most fulfilling things one can do. James Cathey was one of those lucky people who spent his life doing what he loved–taking photographs of rodeo folks and selling them to those competitors. He also wrote articles about various aspects of rodeo, which always included his photos.

When you are passionate about what you do, it isn't work. Every day is a delight, and it seems there are always surprises that open more doors for you than you ever imagined. What makes people who love what they do excel? Cowboys and cowgirls say that when they compete in their chosen events they get an adrenaline rush that is like no other. Could James Cathey have gotten that adrenaline rush when he captured those fantastic shots on film?

James Cathey's family always brought out the camera to document family gatherings such as reunions, and graduations. When he chose mechanical engineering and math in college he never gave photography a thought. But while in the military and at war some of the amazing sights he saw from his plane were breathtaking. Although he had responsibilities to perform, he always wished he could have captured more of those views on camera.

When returning from World War II he needed a job. He had a family to support. He purchased a camera and found that after trial and error taking rodeo photographs from inside the arena, with the action right in front of him, snapping that shot at just the right moment, then running for cover was exhilarating! It didn't take this fast thinking, clever young man long to make his way to the top level of rodeo and be the favored photojournalist in the arena.

During this time he met the young women who were so determined to see that they had a place in rodeo. They had just formed their own organization–Girls Rodeo Association (GRA). He was very impressed with their passion, thoroughness and professionalism in producing All Girl Rodeos. They also competed in the Rodeo Cowboys Association rodeos that he photographed. He quickly got to know many of the girls, and they in turn got to know Cathey, since he was taking their photos as they competed.

When he was offered a position with the GRA to be their first publicity director he couldn't say no. His efforts, and what the members did, moved the GRA slowly across our country. James Cathey became one of the best in his photojournalistic world.

Many of the young women who were founding members of the GRA are no longer with us. Those whom I have talked with who competed in the early days and knew James Cathey had this to say about him:

Dude Barton – "I thought a lot of him. Whatever the girls decided to do, he always went along with them. He published our magazine, and it was full of news and helped us spread across the country. He was always right there with us in the crowd."

Dixie Reger Mosley – "James Cathey was always with the group. He was just one of us, but he was a guy."

Betty Dusek – "James was a good guy and tended to business."

Florence Youree – "I met James at an AJRA rodeo in Post, Texas, and we got acquainted. I always looked forward to his magazine, *Powder Puff and Spurs*. He always covered the All Girl Rodeos and wrote wonderful stories. He was a great benefit to the GRA, and we knew he really cared about us."

When James Cathey and the fledgling GRA met it was obviously meant to be. They needed each other, and both went on to do great things. He created the photography and the words to help them expand their organization, now called the Women's Professional Rodeo Association (WPRA). The girls, in turn, gave him great material and action that opened many new doors for his creativity. It was truly a win-win situation.

While American rodeo has always been fun, entertaining and competitive, it grew out of the hard work and specialized skills of ranching in the West. Ranchers' sons and daughters were often the primary ranch hands, and they naturally became experts at breaking horses, roping, branding, and rounding up cattle. Inevitably, competitions of ranching skills developed between the ranch hands on the individual ranches as well as between neighboring ranches. Later these became a part of local day-long festivals where both men and women participated in many equestrian events and contests.

Most people agree that the first professional rodeo was held sometime around the early 1880s. Whether it was in North Platte, Nebraska; Pecos, Texas; Prescott, Arizona; Alpine, Texas; or some other location is open to considerable debate. According to noted rodeo historian, Gail Hughbanks Woerner, the exact place and date are lost to history.

Thereafter, professional and sometimes shady rodeo producers organized rodeos in many towns where local cowboys and cowgirls competed for money and prizes. In addition to the rodeos, traveling Wild West shows provided entertainment for the crowds. Here, participants exhibited skills in racing, trick riding, steer riding, wild cow milking, and the like, developing huge followings and reputations much like other professional athletes of the day.

All this began to change in 1912, when a group of Calgary businessmen hired American roper Guy Weadick to manage, promote, and produce his first Stampede, an annual celebration that combined a rodeo, contests, exhibitions, and even dancing. Weadick selected the events, determined the rules and eligibility, chose the officials, and invited well-known cowboys and cowgirls to take part. The initial Calgary Stampede was a huge success and led the way for a new era in which powerful producers, not local committees, would come to dominate rodeo and greatly expand its audience.

During this time, women rode broncs and roped steers. They participated in a variety of relay and other races and demonstrated their trick riding and fancy roping skills. In some of these contests, they competed against men and often won.

But then several seemingly unrelated factors conspired to greatly curtail opportunities for women in rodeo. The rise of rodeo as a profession, especially after the 1929 formation of the Rodeo Association of America (RAA) by rodeo owners and their representatives, led to the evolution of rodeo into carefully managed profit-making entertainment, putting more pressure on rodeo promoters to tighten their productions to make them less time consuming and more fan friendly. A tragic accident involving a female rodeo rider at the Pendleton Round-Up, also in 1929, sparked a movement by many of the prominent professional rodeos in the West to ban women from competing in "rough stock" events. The "Depression Years" of the 1930s drove a number of rodeo producers out of business. In 1936, when rodeo cowboys formed the Cowboys Turtle Association (CTA) to represent their interests with rodeo owners and producers, women were not included in the negotiations. Additionally, World War II placed severe hardships on almost all American sports, and rodeo was no exception.

In the 1930s and 1940s, women remained full contestants in the Eastern indoor rodeos, at such independent venues as Madison Square Garden and

Boston Garden. Although they continued to compete alongside men there and at small, mostly amateur rodeos, their opportunities for big-time rodeo stardom were steadily fading.

Texas rodeos led the way in shunting women to the sidelines with their glamorous "sponsor girls," first introduced at the Stamford Cowboy Reunion in 1931. Young ladies, sixteen years or older, were recruited to represent ranches, businesses or Chambers of Commerce. They led the opening day parade, participated in special features of the rodeo, and took part in local social events planned for them. The primary purpose of the sponsor girls was to add a little charm and glamour to the previously masculine rodeo.

Prizes were given to the girl riding the best mount, wearing the most attractive western outfit, and exhibiting the best horsemanship. Horsemanship was subjectively decided by the judges. Regardless of the skills involved, beauty, attire and bloodline were much more important than athletic ability in determining the final winners of sponsor contests.

With the advent of sponsor girl competitions, women assumed more of a supporting role for the rodeo men, and their opportunities to compete in riding and roping began to dwindle, although their ranch work continued.

The year 1942 saw the end of women's bronc riding competitions at both the Madison Square Garden and Boston Garden rodeos. That change in the East almost completed the transition, all across the continent, of rodeo cowgirls from contestants to beautiful props. Consequently, all aspects of female participation decreased significantly between 1943 and 1946. In 1928, one-third of all rodeos had featured women's competitive events. After 1942, an average of just twelve women per year were active in professional rodeo.[1]

However, by 1947 ranch women of a new generation were coming of age. They were strong willed, independent and highly skilled athletes who wanted a chance to compete at the highest level in the one sport that they knew intimately. They had grown up honing the skills that every ranch hand needed to survive and every champion cowboy or cowgirl who had come before them had exhibited in the arena.

This book tells the story of some of the key women who led this new generation of rodeo cowgirls in the incubation, establishment, and development of the Girls Rodeo Association (GRA) from the late 1940s through the early 1950s. With the invaluable assistance of photojournalist James Cathey, one man who championed their cause, they forever changed the course of women's rodeo by launching what is now the Women's Professional Rodeo Association (WPRA), the oldest women's professional sports association in the United States.

Craig W. Cathey

---

1   Mary Lou LeCompte. *Cowgirls of the Rodeo: Pioneer Professional Athletes* (Urbana: U of Illinois Press, 1933), 137-138.

Photo by Ralph R. Doubleday, from the Bruce McCarroll Collection of the Bonnie & Frank McCarroll Rodeo Archives, Dickinson Research Center, National Cowboy & Western Heritage Museum, RC2006.076.107

Rodeo cowgirl Bonnie McCarroll, riding Bear Cat at the Tex Austin Rodeo in Chicago, probably in 1926.

More than anything else, it was the sound of Bonnie McCarroll's head hitting the ground as her horse continued to somersault that told Ollie Osborn something was wrong.

"I could hear that girl's head hit the ground from where I was in the bleachers," Osborn, a Wild West show cowgirl and champion saddle bronc rider, said in an interview about McCarroll decades after her death. The horse bucked at least six times, Bonnie's head hitting the ground each time.[2]

"I thought," she recalled, "'that don't sound right.' And when they went in to pick Bonnie up, the horse stumbled. He didn't go flat down, but he went down to his knees."

Osborn's account of what happened that day was one of dozens that film producer and writer Shirley Morris captured after learning about the role that McCarroll's death played in the history of women's rodeo. There were others, and not one was easy to listen to.

---

2   Shirley Morris, "Horrific Cowgirl Saddle Bronc Wreck 1929 Bonnie McCarroll," August 9, 2011, https://www.youtube.com/watch?v=qtw-t7nvB8g

Photo by W.S. Bowman, from the Bruce McCarroll Collection of the Bonnie & Frank McCarroll Rodeo Archives, Dickinson Research Center, National Cowboy & Western Heritage Museum, RC2006.076.312-1

Bonnie McCarroll in her rough dismount of a bronc named Silver at the 1915 Pendleton Round-Up.

Nineteen-year-old Pendleton rodeo clown Monk Carden, McCarroll's husband Frank, and several other friends and competitors were in the arena or within feet of Bonnie that day. When the snubber, the man whose job it was to remove the bag covering the bronc's eyes, pulled off the blindfold, they all watched in horror as both history and tragedy unfolded in front of them.

The first rider of the day, McCarroll had drawn Black Cat, a horse that Carden described as agitated before McCarroll ever got on him.

McCarroll didn't hesitate. She'd been around agitated horses before.

In fact, fifteen years earlier, rodeo photographer Walter Bowman had taken a picture of McCarroll tumbling off the back of a horse named Silver in her first bronc-busting competition at the Pendleton Round-Up. The image had gone about as viral as it could back in the time before cell phones and the Internet.

McCarroll is shown in Bowman's famous photo headed ground-ward, upside down. Her legs are splayed in the air, her curly hair flying, one gloved hand just touching the hard-packed clay arena as she prepares to hit ground. Silver rears up on his hind legs, his back arched skyward, the remnant of a broken or severed rope hobble visible on one stirrup.[3]

She survived that fall, and fifteen years later, on September 18, 1929, Bonnie returned to the same arena for what was to be her farewell ride before retiring from rodeo.

McCarroll shook her dark brown hair out of her face, pulling it back behind her ears before putting her wide-brimmed felt hat back on her head. Like other famous cowgirls of her day, Tad Lucas, Bea Kirnan, Prairie Rose Henderson, Mabel Strickland, Princess Mohawk, Ruth Roach, Kitty Canutt, and Prairie Lillie, McCarroll was a real champion cowgirl and the fans knew it. True, some of the more urban audiences were uncomfortable watching women bronc busters, but they came anyway.

Before the snubber pulled the blindfold off Black Cat, McCarroll had a lot to look forward to. She was only thirty-four years old at the time, and this would be her farewell ride. She and her husband, Frank, would retire from what had been, by any standard, a long run in an extreme sport. The McCarrolls had thousands of fans, but it was time to put their saddles away—at least when it came to entertaining in them—and enjoy their lives together.

According to witnesses that day, Black Cat was agitated, twitchy, and anxious about being there, but he wouldn't have to wait long. McCarroll was getting ready to ride. She hitched up her pants, tugged at her chaps, and adjusted her worn leather glove. She looked up at Frank, saying, "Please Frank, just one more show. I want Pendleton to be my last ride." She was asking, but she was going to ride regardless. She tugged at the long sleeves of her white cotton blouse, and waited for his reply.

Frank's jaw tightened briefly, then his mouth turned up in the slightest of smiles. He'd urged, even begged her, not to

---

3   Richard Ian Kimball, *Legends Never Die: Athletes and Their Afterlives in Modern America* (Syracuse: Syracuse University Press, 2017), 60.

3

Photographer Unknown, from the Bruce McCarroll Collection of the
Bonnie & Frank McCarroll Rodeo Archives, Dickinson Research Center,
National Cowboy & Western Heritage Museum, RC2006.076.435-1

*Bonnie McCarroll, in a portrait
probably from 1924.*

ride in another show. Today was no different. Ollie Osborn remembered the day.

She said, "Frank, I want to make one more show—just one more show."[4]

"Bonnie, I wish you'd retire," he responded. He wasn't being pushy, just practical.

She smiled at her husband and said, "Frank, I promise this will be my last show." This wasn't the twenty-first century. Women still looked to their husbands for permission—and Frank gave it, as he usually did. "Last one," he said, making it both a question and a promise.

"Last one," she replied. He nodded and off they went.[5]

She finished adjusting her outfit, pulled on her glove, snugged down the leather lace securing it to her wrist, and turned toward the arena. Frank was at her side as she walked out to Black Cat. He lifted her into her saddle, as a parent might lift a child, as was his tradition. The cheers and hooting and hollering of fans began as they recognized the couple. Some of the crowd knew this was her farewell ride; others were simply excited to see her perform again.

In her book *Cowgirls of the Rodeo,* Mary Lou LeCompte notes that more than half of the 190 cowgirls who competed between 1920 and 1936 had careers lasting only three years. McCarroll, rodeo's most famous cowgirl, had a fifteen-year career. She and Frank had pleased crowds up and down the Northwest American rodeo circuit. McCarroll was famous for her agility and tricks as well as her bronc busting. She rarely failed to astound her fans, and she thought today would be no different.

After lifting his wife into her saddle, Frank adjusted her rope hobbles. Hobbles were used by some female bronc riders as a way of tying the stirrups together under the horse. Free stirrups allowed the rider to rise and fall, and spur with each buck.

4 Ibid.
5 Ibid.

There were good and bad aspects to the hobbles. They prolonged the ride, giving the audience more run for their money. The bad side was that a rider using rope hobbles was more or less locked into the saddle, making the ride more dangerous. Hobbles helped shorter or weaker women stay in the saddle longer, but they could hinder a rider's safe dismount. Women had the option to "ride slick," or ride hobbled, but at the 1929 Pendleton Round-Up, hobbles were required. McCarroll didn't have a choice.

"I was there, ten or fifteen yards back of the snubbing horse," Carden recalled. "When they pulled that blindfold off the horse it reared over backwards, with McCarroll still on its back. And when that horse got up, she was still in the saddle. I went over there, something went terribly wrong and Bonnie was just out cold. There was no color in her face. It was just chalk white. We all knew she was hurt bad."

Historian and rodeo performer Reba Perry Blakely had her own memories of the day. "I was there that day," she told Shirley Morris. "I saw how it happened. A pickup rider came in and grabbed Bonnie's right arm, and just as Black Cat was buckling over, his right hand froze on her right arm and then Black Cat did a complete forward somersault. When the horse got back up Bonnie's left boot was still caught in the stirrup, and she was on the ground. And then her head hit the ground with each buck until, mercifully, that boot finally came off."

McCarroll's hobbled boots prevented any chance of escape, even though the pickup rider managed to grab her arm and almost pull her out of her saddle, one foot turned, locking her back in. Each eyewitness saw the horrific event differently. Each account is as valid as the next, each as heartbreaking.

Once McCarroll was on the ground, Frank ran over to her, unbuckled her chaps and rushed her to a waiting car and then to a nearby hospital, where she died eleven days later.

There wasn't much outcry until Pendleton in 1929. McCarroll's death changed things.

The Pendleton Round-Up committee dropped cowgirl bronc riding from its programs, and other rodeos in the Western states soon followed suit.

This tragedy was not the first time a rodeo cowgirl had been seriously injured or killed. Mabel Strickland was reported "near death" after failing to complete a trick at Madison Square Garden's World Series Rodeo in 1926. After winning the title for World Champion Lady Rider at the Cheyenne Frontier Days, Strickland went on to compete in New York.

She was performing a trick in which she was to move under the horse's neck and grab the saddle on the other side as the horse galloped around the arena. She lost her grip and fell beneath the belly of the galloping animal. Strickland recovered from her injuries and even went on to win several more championships. However, Mabel was a popular film star known to millions, the event was widely covered in the news, and some people began to question whether rodeo was truly a sport for women.

At least six cowgirls had died since women started competing in ladies bronc riding in 1904. But there wasn't much outcry until Pendleton in 1929. McCarroll's death changed things. The Pendleton Round-Up committee dropped cowgirl bronc riding from its programs and other rodeos in the Western states soon followed suit. When Bonnie died, the opportunities for cowgirls to compete began to die as well.

Eighteen years would pass before two West Texas ranch girls, Nancy Binford and Thena Mae Farr, teamed up to produce their historic first all-girl rodeo, and almost simultaneously, photojournalist James Cathey launched his remarkable career documenting rodeos with his camera and written words. Together, these two developments forever altered the course of women's rodeo and opened up exciting new opportunities for rodeo cowgirls.

*T*he first decades of the twentieth century are often referred to as the Golden Age of women's rodeo. Female performers such as Fox Hastings, Mabel Strickland, Tad Lucas, and Florence Randolph rode their way to rodeo stardom at Cheyenne's Frontier Days, the Pendleton Round-Up, and the Calgary Stampede or by signing on as contract performers with traveling wild west shows like Buffalo Bill's Wild West, Pawnee Bill's Wild West, or the 101 Ranch Wild West Show. Fort Worth officially started indoor rodeos in 1918 which included events for both men and women. Madison Square Garden (1922) and Boston Garden hosted indoor rodeos that featured women's rough stock contests, and Chicago added its Soldier Field Rodeo in the mid 1920s. In 1928, the height of professional rodeo participation for women, almost one-third of rodeos featured women's competitions.

But in the background, things were changing: unionization and the predictable wages it brought expanded the middle class as unions enabled men's wages to support the family; middle class values emphasized a traditional (read: Victorian) role for women, as seen in more restrictive clothing and emphasis on cosmetics and beauty; and the competitive rodeo cowgirl was slowly replaced by the ranch girl, especially the beautiful, well-dressed girl who supported her man and handled the social responsibilities for the family. Rodeo became big business. Professional rodeo producers needed to control expenses to be profitable, and eliminating separate stock for women's events provided one solution. Cheyenne discontinued female bronc riding in 1928. Bonnie McCarroll's death the following year reignited the controversy over so-called dangerous sports and the proper role for women in society.

Stamford, Texas, originated its Cowboy Reunion in 1930 with no women's events. The next year they created "Sponsor Girls" to add some public appeal.

Rodeo producers banded together in 1929 to found the Rodeo Association of America (RAA) to begin regulating rodeo, standardizing the events, and assuring contestants that RAA rodeos would follow published guidelines. Women's events were never prohibited in these rodeos, nor were they required, but tighter RAA restrictions increased pressure on producers to streamline their productions by reducing the number of events, and women's events fell victim to the reductions.

The 1929 stock market crash and ensuing financial depression devastated many communities. In an attempt to revive its spirits and ignite some town enthusiasm, Stamford, Texas, decided to hold a community-sponsored Cowboy Reunion and celebration over the July 4th weekend. The entire town pitched in to make it happen.

Stamford originated its Cowboy Reunion in 1930 with no women's events. The following year Stamford invited the surrounding communities and local ranches to send girls to compete in a sponsor contest and add to the Cowboy Reunion's appeal. The girls promoted their sponsors, rode in parades, attended social events, and competed for prizes.

However, selection of winners was subjective. Having the best horse or most attractive outfit could be determining factors. Horsemanship was often exhibited by racing through a figure-eight or cloverleaf pattern, but the races were not timed, and there were no specific criteria for winning.

Stamford's 1931 sponsor girls event was a big hit. Audiences enthusiastically cheered the girls, showing that there was a following for girls' rodeo events. The sponsor event expanded to other Texas and Oklahoma rodeos throughout the 1930s and early 1940s, lending glamour and excitement to the otherwise all-male rodeos. In fact, Stamford called their barrel race the "sponsor race." Even so, this gave the cowgirls opportunities, although limited, to continue competing. More importantly, since the same girls were often sponsors at numerous rodeos year after year, they kept in contact with each other, forming friendships that served them well in later years. Sponsor girl events flourished, but competitive rodeo events for women were largely the casualty.

In smaller local community rodeos, women still rode and competed, but the door to larger rodeo fame was closing. What remained were local rodeos, roping contests, sponsor contests at the RAA-sanctioned rodeos, matched roping events, sometimes held in conjunction with those rodeos, and opportunities for girls to meet and form friendships with other sponsor girls.

Women did, however, continue competing in the Eastern rodeos, with Vivian White winning the last saddle bronc championship held at Madison Square Garden in 1941.

In the early 1940s, several strong, independent women attempted to produce all-girl rodeos. In northeast Texas, Fay Kirkwood produced the Bonham Girls Rodeo on June 26–29, 1942, with a definite patriotic theme. Local girls participated in sponsor contests and cowgirls performed exhibitions rather than competing in professional competitions. Kirkwood's flair for publicity created considerable interest, and Bonham supported her well.

Kirkwood scheduled a second girls rodeo—with women competing in eight contests, four of which were exhibitions—for late July in Wichita Falls. Again there was a patriotic theme. Contestants came from all over. Dude Barton took home multiple awards, her local newspaper reporting that the only reason she didn't win Sheppard Air Force Base was that Kirkwood didn't offer it as a prize.

In September, Vaughn Krieg Huskey produced a third rodeo: the Flying V All Cow-Girl Rodeo in Paris, Texas, again with a patriotic theme. This rodeo was even more tilted toward professional cowgirls and attracted a good cadre of top women contestants.

By 1943 essential resources for the war were becoming increasingly scarce, and gas and rubber rationing were strict. Many communities moth-balled their rodeos during the remainder of World War II. Local competitions continued, but with automobile driving sharply curtailed, the few women who continued to appear in rodeos often did so as contract performers, such as trick riders and ropers for established rodeos or traveling shows. Others went to work in war-related industries or filled jobs that GIs had vacated when called to war. Dorothy McDonald Barnes switched to a typewriter in 1943, while Tad Lucas and Reba Perry Blakely built airplanes.

The war turned male ranch hands into soldiers. Many women's ranch responsibilities increased and further honed their skills. For a while, the RAA loosened its rules to allow more women's events in rodeos, and girls responded.

As the war wound down and GIs began returning home, rodeos started to rebound, attendance boomed and the RAA reverted to its pre-war rules. But girls still wanted to compete, and they sought more rodeo opportunities. Participation in sponsor contests expanded markedly. Some sponsor events were being timed, and it became more common for rodeos to include two events for girls. In 1944 and 1945, L.A. Worthington of the West Fork Ranch, father of Jackie, Mary, and Ada, produced rodeos in which girls rode—Jackie gave bull riding and bareback bronc exhibitions—in addition to the sponsor girls contest.

The 1945 Stamford Cowboy Reunion drew almost forty girls, as did Stamford's 1946 and 1947 Reunions. In July 1947, the West of the Pecos Rodeo attracted fifty sponsor entries. It was there that the girls first discussed the possibility of joining together in what would later become the Girls Rodeo Association (GRA).

Photo by Rodney_X/ASlamy.com

Photo by U.S. Army, provided by the Cathey family.

A s James Cathey looked out from his B-17 "Flying Fortress" at the snow-covered countryside passing 20,000 feet below, he viewed the tops of white clouds that looked almost like more snow. He reached for the machine gun mount to steady himself and gazed at the large formation of war machines passing through what he suddenly saw as a serene, almost heavenly scene. Momentarily entranced by the ironic beauty, he lost all awareness of roaring engines and the bone-freezing cold. An avid amateur photographer, he nearly reached for his camera, but new sounds of aerial explosions from anti-aircraft defenses jerked him back to reality.

The eldest of seven children, James was born in 1917 on a rural plot of land near Tell, a small speck of a town, just west of Childress, in the southeast corner of the Texas Panhandle. There, on the farm and cattle ranch established by his great-grandfather in the 1880s, James grew up in a large extended family of uncles, aunts and cousins.

Whether at their frequent gatherings or on group driving trips to natural wonders like Palo Duro Canyon or the mountains of Colorado, someone was always carrying a camera and creating photo memories for the family. For James, sharing photographs was a natural part of life.

A rural West Texas boy, James loved being outdoors, working with animals and crops. Upon graduating from Childress High School in 1935, he joined the Civilian Conservation Corps (CCC), building roads and park facilities in New Mexico. Later, he attended Colorado A&M in Fort Collins, studying mechanical engineering and forest management. He envisioned a career as an outdoorsman rooted somewhere on the slopes of the Rocky Mountains.

In early 1943, James put that career plan on hold. He had married his best friend's sister, Margie Elease Johnson, a pretty North Texas farm girl, was soon to become a father, and had enlisted in the Army Air Corps. Everything was changing for him.

Cathey volunteered for bomber duty because that's where the action was, and that's where he always wanted to be: in the center of it all. As his crew's flight engineer and top gunner with the Eighth Air Force's 306th Bombardment Group, known as "The Reich Wreckers," he certainly had been at the center of the action in 1944. Now it was February of 1945, and James was on his thirty-fifth and final combat mission.

Although he missed getting a picture of that surreal view on his last mission, because war abruptly got in the way, James had been developing his photographic skills during his tour of duty. Having taken pictures most of his life, he packed his old familiar Kodak camera when he shipped to England, and his talent for capturing impressive images became known around the air base. His crew members and other airmen often requested prints to send home to their families, and James realized he was quite good at the art. He enjoyed the special attention it brought and began to think seriously about changing directions to pursue a career in something artistic that really caught his imagination.

Awarded the Air Medal, for "heroism or meritorious achievement," with five oak leaf clusters, signifying receipt of the same high honor six times during his thirty-five missions, Cathey returned home in April, 1945, a highly-decorated airman, seeking a new beginning. He rejoined his young family and moved to Fort Worth, where there were ample career opportunities.

Fully determined to become a professional photographer, he made a significant commitment to the future with the purchase of a Graflex Speed Graphic 4x5 camera, even before finding a job. The Speed Graphic was the camera of choice for most professional news photographers of that day, and he wanted to be well-equipped for stepping into his new career.

James went straight to the major newspapers and applied for a job as a news photographer—with no news experience. All he took to the interviews were his considerable raw talent, a can-do attitude and a professional's camera.

The *Fort Worth Press* opened the door for him, but only as a freelance contractor, paid for photos used. Early on, his new editor told him to make sure every picture tells a story, adding, "If I can't see the story, I can't run with it," a challenge and a guideline that James never forgot.

Being self-taught and lacking professional training might have seemed an obstacle, but it was a special advantage for James. He had learned to see life from his own personal perspective, rather than through the academic filter that many other professionals had been taught. His study of math and mechanical engineering proved to be exactly the background he needed as a photographer working with a complicated, fully adjustable camera. His talent for capturing action, married with good camera work, would eventually take him to places beyond the reach of most of his contemporaries.

It didn't take long for James to learn that news photography was demanding work. He kept a police-band radio in the family's dining room and responded to every call that

His talent for capturing action, married with good camera work, would eventually take him to places beyond the reach of most of his contemporaries.

sounded like a photo opportunity. Every picture that made the *Press* was money for his small family, but his newspaper pay wasn't what he had hoped.

He tried other money-making ideas: taking pictures of homes in upscale neighborhoods after a rare Fort Worth snowstorm, and selling prints to the homeowners to use for Christmas cards; contracting to photograph the staff, facilities and important events for churches, civic clubs and private schools; or showing up at local sporting events, such as Little League baseball games, camera in-hand, and offering to take team pictures or action shots of the kids. Each idea added some income here and there, but none seemed to offer much toward developing the career he envisioned.

Through the struggles, James knew that he had made the right decision in becoming a photographer. He just needed to find his own place within the profession, and he needed subject matter that he could feel passionate about.

In late September of 1947, James headed to Arlington Downs, a horse racing and rodeo venue about twenty minutes east of where he lived in east Fort Worth, to photograph his first professional rodeo.

In the 1940s, rodeo was a very popular and quickly growing sport, actually drawing more paying fans than other professional sports like baseball or football, especially in the Western states. When "the boys" came home from war, rodeos seemed to spring up everywhere. Every town wanted its own rodeo, and Arlington had a good one, where members of the Rodeo Cowboys Association (RCA) came to compete.

Cathey's "PRESS" badge gave him easy access to every corner of the Arlington Downs rodeo grounds, and he was soon inside the arena taking close-ups of the rodeo action.

Standing directly in front of the bucking chutes with an eye trained through a viewfinder—aim, click, and hurry to get out of the way!—was obviously dangerous and very exciting. James felt the rush and realized he was where he

James Cathey photo–2015.006.2.4.42

Margie Cathey, on the left, showing Cathey's photo proofs from the previous rodeo performance and taking print orders in the horse barns adjacent to the Will Rogers Coliseum at the Fort Worth Stock Show and Rodeo, February, 1949.

wanted to be that evening, right in the center of the action. He thought, "Surely the *Press* and the *Arlington News* will grab up some of these great shots!"

Eager to see the results of his night's work, James rushed home, glad that he had planned ahead. Knowing this was a multi-day rodeo, he had his darkroom equipment and chemicals ready for his late night arrival. He got right to work processing the film negatives, enlarging the images to 8x10 proof prints, and binding them into a sample book for showing his pictures to the rodeo promoters and contestants the following evening.

The multi-step process went slowly, taking most of the remaining nighttime hours, but the results surprised even the photographer. He had taken the shots at night, but his closeness to the action enabled his flash bulbs to light every contestant and every animal, and his own natural sense of timing captured action at the peak so well that he could, indeed, see the stories. He could see what came before and what would follow each stop-action image.

At the next evening's performance, James had his proof prints from the first night with him, or rather with Margie. She found a good spot just outside the arena, beside the bucking chutes, to wave down the cowboys and cowgirls who passed her way. "Hi, would you like to see these?" She was pretty, looked even younger than her twenty-five years, and her eyes sparkled with a winning country-girl smile. It wasn't long before a group gathered around her. James was back in the arena with his camera, and Margie was taking more print orders than she could believe.

At that first rodeo, Cathey realized that he could shoot and sell more action photos to rodeo contestants in a couple of days than he could sell to the newspapers in a month.

The Death Drag: What Tad Lucas called her "Back Drag," many called a "Tail Drag," and some dramatic announcers told the fans it was a "Death Drag!" The only way up from the back-bending, head-dizzying position was a powerful abdomen-straining sit-up with the horse continuing its race around the arena. There were no handles until Tad reached all the way up to the saddle. At the Fort Worth Rodeo in 1948 Tad was 45 years old and smiling about putting on yet another great show for her hometown crowd.

James was excited about what he was finding out about himself, about his photography and about the thrill of being intimately involved with rodeo. He just had to find another one right away, which wasn't hard to do from Fort Worth. He soon made his way to the Midway rodeo in Stephenville and the Cowtown indoor rodeo in Fort Worth's North Side Coliseum. At each one, he took his place directly in front of the chutes and got in close to the action.

James absolutely loved what he was doing and knew this passion would drive his career. When he arrived at the Cowtown rodeo, he had already dropped the crutch of the "PRESS" badge and was calling himself "the rodeo photographer." That description and his confident walk with his camera got him into where he wanted to be.

People were amazed at how intimate and alive his pictures were. A James Cathey image placed the viewer close to the broncs, the bulls and the riders, almost close enough to touch—maybe dangerously close!

Armed with a number of outstanding samples from photographing his first rodeos, James decided it was time to once again step up into the center of the action. At that time, the Southwestern Exposition and Livestock Show, commonly known as the Fort Worth Stock Show and Rodeo, was one of the largest and most prestigious rodeo events in the country. It was not only credited with producing the first indoor rodeo and being the longest, continuously running rodeo event in America, it was also a major stop on the RCA rodeo circuit. With the RCA headquarters also based in Fort Worth, it was definitely in the center of the action. So, James applied for and won the contract to be "Official Photographer" of the big Fort Worth RCA Rodeo, opening in January of 1948. While most outdoor rodeos allowed several photographers into the arena, seemingly requiring

James Cathey photo–2015.006.233

only a camera and maybe a press pass, the Fort Worth Rodeo was inside the Will Rogers Memorial Coliseum, with only a single arena photographer, who supplied the rodeo committee with all the news release images they needed. Not only was this contract a significant rodeo credential for boosting his new career, but it gave James exclusive arena access, right down front with the bucking stock, his favorite place, where he could capture the action and tell the stories from up close.

James didn't yet know that the 1948 Fort Worth Rodeo would be where he captured one of the most outstanding action shots ever made of the famous "First Lady of Rodeo," Tad Lucas, in her signature "Back Drag" trick ride. There, with her head just inches from the flying rear hooves of her favorite paint horse, was the enthusiastically smiling face of the 45-year-old rodeo star, obviously enjoying yet another show of her skills at entertaining the crowds.

This widely acclaimed James Cathey action photo captures the famous First Lady of Rodeo, Tad Lucas, on Candy Lamb, in her signature "Back Drag" at the 1948 Fort Worth Stock Show and Rodeo. A large print of this image now hangs in the National Cowgirl Museum and Hall of Fame in Fort Worth.

Equipped with a Graflex Speed Graphic camera, loaded with a single 4x5 negative to grant only one chance at any shot, Cathey captured this and other up-close rodeo action photos with disposable flash bulbs and without the aid of a telephoto lens.

James didn't yet know that his iconic photo would, many years later, hang in a position of honor in the National Cowgirl Museum and Hall of Fame, just a short walk from the rodeo arena where it was taken, where Tad Lucas, with James Cathey's help, still amazes the fans.

James didn't yet know that he and Tad, who also called Fort Worth home, would develop a friendship that affected the course of not only his career but also the place of women in professional rodeo.

What James did know was that he had found his passion. He had created his own place, exactly where he wanted to be. He was centered, he was excited, and he knew he had just signed a major-league contract.

As the rodeo opened for its first 1948 performance, James picked up his leather bag of flash bulbs and pre-loaded film carriers and passed its strap over his head to hang it diagonally from his left shoulder to right hip. He put on his hat and pinched the front of the brim to give it a snugging tug, looked up at the crowd and the coliseum lights, and felt a quick flash of warmth, thinking, "I LOVE this!" He turned and smiled at Margie, who was handing him his camera, just as the announcer's voice shook the coliseum with "Let's go! Let's show! Let's RODEO!"

And then, James Cathey entered the arena.

n 1947, Amarillo's Tri-State Fair suddenly had no rodeo. The Will Rogers Range Riders, producers of a fall rodeo for the past four years, had moved their rodeo to mid-summer. This would be the first fair held since it had been mothballed in 1941, and large crowds were expected.

Two West Texas ranch girls stepped in to fill the void. Nancy Binford of Wildorado and Thena Mae Farr of Seymour saw a perfect opportunity to produce an all-girl rodeo and grabbed the chance that fell into their laps. Then they made a run into the history books of women's rodeo.

Founded in 1923, the Tri-State Fair attracted participants from all over West Texas, Oklahoma, and New Mexico. Amarillo business-men had always been enthusi-astic promoters of this annual fall event that brought tens of thousands of attendees to the area while also generating favorable publicity and considerable revenue for the city.

Nancy, the Will Rogers Range Riders' Sweetheart, and her close friend Thena Mae, Miss Seymour, were experienced rodeo "sponsor girls." Sponsor girls were young ladies who were chosen to represent ranches, businesses or Chambers of Commerce in rodeo events, competing for prizes based

Women's rodeo history was redirected in 1947 by these two West Texas ranch girls,

James Cathey photo–2015.006.Binford

James Cathey photo–2015.006.Farr

Nancy Binford (l.) and Thena Mae Farr (r.), when they sold the idea of an all-girl rodeo, produced and managed by themselves, to the committee of Amarillo's Tri-State Fair.

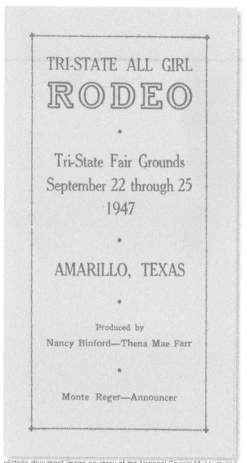

TRI-STATE ALL GIRL

RODEO

•

Tri-State Fair Grounds
September 22 through 25
1947

•

AMARILLO, TEXAS

•

Produced by
Nancy Binford—Thena Mae Farr

•

Monte Reger—Announcer

Historic document image courtesy of the National Cowgirl Museum and
Hall of Fame, Fort Worth, Texas

The call went out, and cowgirls from several states enthusiastically answered, eager for the chance to compete in a rodeo of their own.

primarily upon subjective evaluations of their mounts, riding costumes and equestrian skills.

Nancy and Thena Mae were good at promoting their sponsors. They had become public relations experts, presiding over teas and luncheons, and participating in sponsor dances. They acquired sophistication from competing and winning while observing and learning what constituted a well-organized and well-run rodeo. They also met many important people who taught them how to manage the various components of a rodeo. These two ranch women had attended college, honing their leadership skills in physical education departments still segregated by gender so that women managed the activities and led the organizations. During their extensive experience as sponsor girls they had also met and formed friendships with many other ranch girls, creating the community from which they would draw the competitors for their Tri-State All Girl Rodeo. They were well prepared.

Nancy and Thena Mae presented their idea to the Amarillo Chamber of Commerce. The Chamber, at first somewhat skeptical, approved their request, and the Texas State Fair Board signed on to help advertise and promote the upcoming rodeo.[6] The girls signed the contract on August 21 and immediately put 100 percent of their energy into creating a roaring success for the fair and opening new opportunities for rodeo cowgirls.

Up and down Polk Street strode the producers, soliciting prizes and donations for the rodeo. Interview here. Interview there. Photo ops and publicity in the local newspapers. Interviews with dignitaries. Smiles for everyone. Invitations to send sponsor girls—yes, but this time the sponsor girl contest would be decided by timing alone. No more best costume or prettiest hairdo or richest dad, just their equestrian skills!

6   Renée M. Laegreid, "Ranch Women and Rodeo Performers in Post—World War II West Texas," in *Texas Women: Their Histories, Their Lives* (Athens, GA: University of Georgia Press, 2015), 341–42.

James Cathey photo–2015.006.4.7.0.28

Cowgirls from Texas, New Mexico, Oklahoma and as far away as California supported the rodeo. They jumped at the chance to compete in a full range of events: bull and bareback bronc riding, saddle bronc, calf roping, team roping, cutting, ribbon racing, and barrel racing. Entries poured in.

This would be the first competitive all-girl rodeo: the first rodeo produced and staffed by women with all female contestants. With the exception of renowned announcer Monte Reger and a couple of pick-up men, girls handled everything. Even the clown, Dixie Reger, was from their list of all-girl contestants. In addition to competing in several events, Dixie and her sister Virginia entertained as trick riders and ropers, with Virginia thrilling the crowd as she sailed over a car on her mount. Nancy later remarked that they couldn't have put on the rodeo without the Reger family.

Nancy and Thena Mae planned their rodeo to appeal to a broad audience and to attract the paying spectators they needed to be successful. They promoted the cowgirls as both athletic cowhands and traditional women who were married, managed their homes, and cared for their families. The two of them were photographed riding horses, but also in the kitchen cooking. They managed the myriad of details with aplomb.

Amarillo was ready for the fair, and the talk was that this new rodeo would be something to behold. Widespread publicity fanned the pent-up demand for the fair and brought a crowd of 150,000 out to line the parade route, as reported by *Lubbock Avalanche* and *Amarillo Daily News*.

Virginia Reger, seen here at the 1950 Belton, Texas, All Girl Rodeo, performed this same signature feat to the amazement of the fans at the 1947 Tri-State All Girl Rodeo.

James Cathey photo–2015.006.9.22.9.10

Jackie Worthington showing the winning bull riding skills that she brought to the first all-girl rodeo at Amarillo's 1947 Tri-State Fair, competes at the 1949 Fort Smith, Arkansas All Girl Rodeo. Jackie is wearing her trophy chaps won at the Tri-State. Lettering at the waist says "TRI-STATE," down the left leg is "AMARILLO 1947," and down the right is "ALL GIRL RODEO."

The rough-riding cowgirls at the GRA's All Girl Rodeos rode steers in the bucking event that they called "bull riding." Although some refer to it as "steer riding," throughout this book we adhere to the GRA's preference of "bull riding."

Guns went off, balloons went up, and the Shamrock Band resumed its former role of opening the fair. Then Amarillo's own Will Rogers Range Riders, the fifty-strong mounted troupe, rode down Polk Street, followed by twenty-plus sponsor girls, merchant and organization floats, thirty cowgirl contestants dressed in their best western outfits, and marching bands from several area high schools.

Opening day, September 23, as the grand-entry parade brought in the colors with the American and Lone Star flags carried at a full gallop for the entire length of the arena, frenetic cheering erupted, proving Nancy and Thena Mae's vision had been spot on. There were over seventy-five entrants in the various events, and every event was well-contested. Nancy commented on the calf roping: "We had eight

22

ropers out the first day, some of them had never thrown a rope in an arena, and there wasn't a calf missed."[7]

The stands were packed to cheer Jackie Worthington completing her eight-second Brahma bull ride in style. Madison Square Garden's last champion cowgirl bronc rider, Vivian White, thrilled the crowds with her winning ride. Announcer Monte Reger had to continually remind the standing-room-only crowd not to block the views. Usually fences protect the people from the animals—this time, the fences protected the cowgirls from their enthusiastic fans. Area newspapers eagerly reported each day's winners, often proudly highlighting their "own" cowgirl's accomplishments. Rodeo crowds increased at each performance with the final day topping 4,200. The grandstands overflowed and standees filled any open space. The rodeo was indeed a success.

When the final results were tabulated, Fern Sawyer, of Crossroads, New Mexico, had won Best All-Around Cowgirl, although she was bested in her signature cutting event by seventeen-year-old Jerry Ann Portwood of Fort Worth. Dude Barton of Flomot, Texas, captured the calf roping and barrel racing titles, Jackie Worthington, of Jacksboro, Texas, won bull riding and bareback bronc, and Fern Sawyer took team roping.

The Tri-State Fair Association cited the All Girl Rodeo as the highlight of the fair. It contributed $1,885 in profits to the fair's reserve fund, and they welcomed it back for 1948.

A significant result of Nancy and Thena Mae's successful all-girl rodeo came from a controversy that developed during the tie-down calf roping competition. This contributed to the formation of the Girls Rodeo Association in early 1948.

According to Jackie Worthington, holder of twenty-three world championships in professional women's rodeo, this is how the organization of the GRA came about:

> *"We had eight ropers out the first day, and some of them had never thrown a rope in an arena, and there wasn't a calf missed. They were real excited about it, and it turned out real well."*
>
> — Nancy Binford, recalling the 1947 Tri-State Rodeo in a 1985 interview.

---

7   Renée M. Laegreid, *Riding Pretty: Rodeo Royalty in the American West* (Lincoln: University of Nebraska Press, 2006), 190.

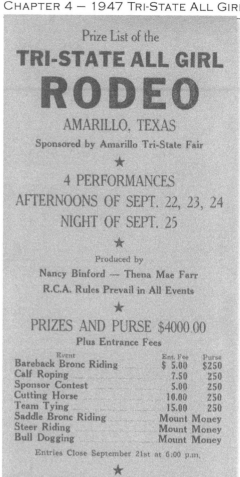

Prize List of the
TRI-STATE ALL GIRL
RODEO
AMARILLO, TEXAS
Sponsored by Amarillo Tri-State Fair

★

4 PERFORMANCES
AFTERNOONS OF SEPT. 22, 23, 24
NIGHT OF SEPT. 25

★

Produced by
Nancy Binford — Thena Mae Farr
R.C.A. Rules Prevail in All Events

★

PRIZES AND PURSE $4000.00
Plus Entrance Fees

Event	Ent. Fee	Purse
Bareback Bronc Riding	$ 5.00	$250
Calf Roping	7.50	250
Sponsor Contest	5.00	250
Cutting Horse	10.00	250
Team Tying	15.00	250
Saddle Bronc Riding		Mount Money
Steer Riding		Mount Money
Bull Dogging		Mount Money

Entries Close September 21st at 6:00 p.m.

★

MONTE REGER—Arena Secretary and Announcer

★

Address Correspondence to:
Tri-State All Girl Rodeo, Amarillo, Texas

Historic document image courtesy of the National Cowgirl Museum and Hall of Fame, Fort Worth, Texas

Some rough-stock events were included only as crowd-pleasing exhibitions at the 1947 Tri-State. The "Mount Money" was paid to each cowgirl who volunteered. Future National Cowgirl Hall of Fame member Fern Sawyer rode a steer for $7 against her father's wishes. She held on so tightly that the rope broke her hand in nine places. She said her daddy wasn't too happy about it, because she got $7 in mount money, and it cost him $1,000 to have her hand fixed.

"All of us there at Amarillo roped the way the cowboys did. If the calf was down when we got to it, we would get it to its feet and throw it before we tied it. This one girl roped her calf, and when she got to it, it was lying down. She just got down and tied it, which made her a lot faster than anybody else. When we complained to the judge that she couldn't do it that way, he told us that we didn't have any rules that said she couldn't. There were no guidelines for him to go by, so he let her time stand.

We decided right then that we needed to organize, set rules, and elect officers. Since we had girls from all over the country there at the Amarillo rodeo, we called a meeting for the following February and drafted a set of rules and bylaws and elected officers."[8]

"I remember having an all-girl rodeo in Amarillo in late 1947 and then we all decided to meet in San Angelo in 1948, and the GRA was formed."[9]
—Dixie Reger Mosley

"We were just sick of being cheated and having no rules. We were ready for some organization—honestly, just to make things better."[10]
—Betty Barron Dusek

"At the Amarillo all-girl rodeo in September, a group of us met and decided we wanted an association. We elected Margaret Owens as our representative. Margaret called the February 28 meeting at the San Angelus Hotel in San Angelo."[11]
—Blanche Altizer Smith

8   Margaret Owens, *Girls Rodeo Magazine*, 1977, 12.
9   Laura Lambert, "Where Are They Now? The History Behind the Jumping Cowgirl: The Life of Dixie Reger," *WPRA NEWS*, June 2017, 46–47.
10 Laura Lambert, "Where Are They Now? Betty Dusek - Paving the Way," *WPRA NEWS*, May 2017, 46.
11 Blanche Altizer Smith, "The Girls Rodeo Association," *Western Horseman*, July 1953, 12.

James Cathey photo–2015.006.5.2.22

And so, on Saturday afternoon, February 28, the Girls Rodeo Association held its founding meeting. Thirty-eight women responded, the majority of them being rodeo cowgirl contestants and performers. Their main purpose was to standardize rodeo rules applying to women and to eliminate unfair practices. In the past, rules had too often been changed at the last minute, and girls never knew exactly what they would be required to do. In addition, sometimes advertised prizes were never paid. As Margaret Owens Montgomery put it: "We intend to work with the rodeo management so that there will be complete understanding. If you know what you will do in a rodeo contest before you even go there, then there won't be any reason for argument."

Margaret Owens Montgomery was elected president, Dude Barton vice president, Mrs. Sid Pearson secretary-treasurer, and Sug Owens publicity director. Jackie Worthington was selected as the general chairman of directors of the various competitive events.

The GRA adopted contest rules that generally followed those of the Rodeo Cowboys Association. Dues were set at $10.00 per year, and the rules were set to take effect on May 1, 1948.

The best of the 1947 Tri-State barrel racers, Dude Barton shows her tight barrel hugging at the 1949 Santa Rosa Round-Up, Vernon, Texas.

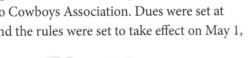

James Cathey photo–2015.006.4.6.0.3

Margaret Owens Montgomery, the first president of the Girls Rodeo Association, at the 1950 Belton All Girl Rodeo.

While the GRA adopted RCA rules to govern most of their events, one rule that they wrote for themselves was that a rider need not keep a free hand in the competitive bucking events of bareback bronc riding and bull riding. A cowgirl could hold on with two hands. The free hand rule was kept for the GRA's saddle bronc riders.

*F*ort Worth, Texas, was rodeo central for the western and central plains in the late 1940s and early 1950s. Not only was Fort Worth James Cathey's new hometown, it was national rodeo headquarters for all of North America. The city's rodeo history had begun in 1896 at the site of the stockyards in North Fort Worth. The famous indoor rodeos at the North Side Coliseum began in 1908 and the nation's first indoor professional rodeo was held there in 1918.

The Will Rogers Memorial Coliseum, with its huge indoor rodeo arena, became home to the Fort Worth Rodeo beginning in 1944.

The Cowboys' Turtle Association, which had formed in 1936 as a union representing professional rodeo cowboys, held a restructuring meeting in Fort Worth in 1945. There they developed a new set of rules and regulations governing the sport, changed the name of the organization to Rodeo Cowboys Association, elected Toots Mansfield of Bandera, Texas, as president, and established a new headquarters in the Sinclair Building downtown.

It would be the Livestock Exchange Building, in the Stockyards area, adjacent to the North Side Coliseum, that would become the rodeo command center, and the center of action for Cathey. In January 1949, following a very promising year of photographing rodeos, he opened his first real office and photo studio on the ground floor of the Livestock Exchange, right off the main lobby. Once again,

Photo from Typhoonski, iStock ID 539342128

Fort Worth Livestock Exchange, is located in the Fort Worth Stockyards district. Erected in 1902, the historic building still houses offices. In the 1940s and early '50s it was at the very heart of rodeo central, and it was the home office of James Cathey and of the Girls Rodeo Association.

Photo by Margie Cathey, from the Cathey family's collection, circa 1949

Cathey shows that he has camera, will travel, as he poses for his own promotional photo in front of Fort Worth's iconic Will Rogers Memorial Center, home of the Fort Worth Stock Show and Rodeo, where Cathey got his first big-league break in his rapidly-rising rodeo career.

his knack for finding the core of a story would come into play, propelling him into photographic history.

Throughout 1948 and 1949, Cathey's business was growing rapidly and he was growing closer to the GRA.

The success of the 1947 Tri-State All Girl Rodeo had encouraged the girls to organize, establish a set of rules and formally charter the GRA in February of 1948. They spent most of the rest of the year seeking opportunities to get GRA-approved events included in existing RCA rodeos that were already scheduled and being produced by non-GRA producers. That first year, they had seventy-four paying members and they needed to find rodeos where those girls could compete in events which were in keeping with their newly adopted rules.

Hard work and excellent PR efforts paid off as GRA members participated in a total of sixty events in 1948, made possible in part by the group's two new all-girl rodeos: San Angelo in early summer and Amarillo in October.

Many of the GRA stars began showing up as contestants in events at RCA rodeos which Cathey was photographing. He had become friends with fellow Fort Worth resident Tad Lucas, and she encouraged him to take more pictures of the girls when they performed. She said things like, "We don't even have enough good photographs to promote an all-girl rodeo," or "These girls are excellent athletes and really fine horsewomen who just want a chance to compete, but they need some support, their entry fees just don't cut it. They need to be able to attract more sponsors so that the prize money will at least cover their expenses."

James got his first opportunity to see a significant number of the GRA stars in action when they showed up, some twenty-strong, to compete at the Santa Rosa Round-Up at Vernon, Texas, in May of 1949. As the newly designated "official photographer" of the Round-Up, he was solidly impressed with the girls' athletic skills and profession-alism, and thoroughly documented their performances. A group

James Cathey photo–2015.006.5.2.25

Nancy Binford at the 1949 Santa Rosa Round-Up, Vernon, Texas.

shot of most of the ladies at that rodeo appears on the cover of this book. Tad convinced James to help when he could, but his booming business demanded time. In addition to his major rodeos like Fort Worth and the Santa Rosa Round-Up, scores of other rodeos and horse shows were begging for a photographer of his caliber to cover their events.

Adding to his workload, Cathey was developing into a sought-after photojournalist and accepted a number of regular writing assignments related to his photography of rodeos and horse shows. He became Associate Editor of *Back in the Saddle* magazine, writing a twice-monthly column, "Rodeo Roundup." He was also a frequent contributing editor for *Western Horseman, Hoofs & Horns,* and the *American Quarter Horse Journal.* They all desired his regular contributions.

As any champion cowboy or cowgirl can tell you, if you want to rise to the top of your profession, you have to become a real "road warrior," constantly traveling from one event to the next. You can't come out on top of the season-long standings unless you amass the most points, and the key to amassing the most points is competing in as many rodeos as possible.

James Cathey photo–2015.006.5.2.28

Thena Mae Farr makes an impressive barrel run at the 1949 Santa Rosa Round-Up, Vernon, Texas.

Life is little different for a top rodeo photographer, and Cathey was determined to excel at his profession. From Fort Worth to Waco, Breckenridge to Ranger, Colorado City to Dublin, Tulsa to Abilene, Bonham to Dallas, Carlsbad to Amarillo, Weatherford to Colorado Springs, James was constantly on the road, following his dream.

Meanwhile, the girls of the GRA were chasing their own dreams.

Although the girls were highly competitive inside the arena, the competition was never just about winning. And it certainly wasn't about money, because there was no money

In 1918 Fort Worth was the home of the first indoor professional rodeo, and in 1950 the city that is still known as "Cowtown" was the home of the Rodeo Cowboys Association and the Girls Rodeo Association. Today Fort Worth is the home of that same first indoor rodeo, of the Texas Rodeo Cowboy Hall of Fame, of the Bull Riding Hall of Fame, of the National Cowgirl Museum and Hall of Fame, of the National Cutting Horse Association, of the American Paint Horse Association, and of Western Horseman *magazine.*

to speak of in those days. It was about the love of competing at something they were all good at, sharing a lifestyle they loved, and, most of all, enjoying the camaraderie of good friends. "It never really mattered who won," said Dude Barton, "we were all just having a good time." "Of course we all wanted to win," echoed Dixie Reger Mosley, "but if another girl needed anything we would all help her out, even if it meant that she could then beat you riding your own horse." "We were like a sisterhood," said Betty Dusek, "we cared about each other and we cared about keeping the GRA going, because without it we wouldn't have been able to compete."[12]

Fort Worth's own, Tad Lucas was a saddle bronc rider and fancy trick rider of great renown. An admirer of James Cathey's talents, she was instrumental in bringing Cathey and the GRA together.

12 2018 interviews with Barton, Reger Mosley and Dusek

James Cathey photo–2015.006.Lucas

Faye Blessing leans into her Hippodrome Stand at a full run at the 1949 Santa Rosa Round-Up, Vernon, Texas. Fey was a frequent stand-in for Hollywood actress Betty Grable.

Chapter 6 — Lawton and Beyond

*I*t all came together for James Cathey and the Girls Rodeo Association in Lawton, Oklahoma, in August 1949. Throughout 1948 and most of 1949, at the urging of Tad Lucas and the GRA's first president, Margaret Owens Montgomery, James had been working more and more closely with the GRA as they built an increasing presence in the RCA rodeos he was photographing.

For James, this was an extremely busy time. In addition to numerous horse shows and other horsemanship competitions, he worked more than thirty rodeos in the months prior to the Lawton All Girl Rodeo. Although many of those rodeos included GRA-sanctioned events, Lawton would be Cathey's first all-girl rodeo. His schedule leading up to the opening of Lawton on August 29, 1949, was brutal. On June 25, he was wrapping up the Cowtown Rodeo in Fort Worth. Then it went something like this:

- July 1–8, Amarillo Rodeo, Texas
- July 9–10, Hugo Rodeo, Oklahoma
- July 11–15, Chickasha Rodeo, Oklahoma
- July 20–23, Ranger Rodeo, Texas
- July 27–30, Weatherford Rodeo, Texas
- August 4–5, Monte Vista Rodeo, Colorado
- August 9–13, Colorado Springs Rodeo, Colorado
- August 24–27, Colorado City Rodeo, Texas
- August 29, Opening of Lawton All Girl Rodeo

To say that Cathey was a little road weary as he rolled into Lawton on that Monday afternoon, just hours before the opening of the GRA's three-day rodeo, would be an understatement. When he left Colorado City, Texas, the day before, he could easily have turned the wheels of his Chevrolet

33

By the end of 1949, the GRA was increasing in popularity and expanding from being a Texas-centric organization, becoming more of a regional presence.

wagon toward Fort Worth for the comfort and relaxation that a few days of sleeping at home in his own bed would have provided. But he had promised the GRA that he would do whatever he could to help keep the momentum of the organization moving forward.

Although Lawton would be his first all-girl rodeo, James had spent the entire season watching these women compete at other rodeos, admiring not only their athletic skills, but also the professional way they ran their association. He knew they would put on a great show and he wanted to be there. Even more, he wanted his camera lens to capture the excitement.

Neither Cathey nor his camera were disappointed. By the end of the three-day Lawton rodeo, he was committed to dedicating a significant portion of his time and professional attention to promoting the GRA. Before leaving town for his next rodeos in Woodward and then Elk City, Oklahoma, James committed to serving as the official photographer at the September all-girl rodeo in Fort Smith, Arkansas, and at the GRA National Finals in Corpus Christi in October.

By the end of 1949, the GRA was increasing in popularity and expanding from being a Texas-centric organization, becoming more of a regional presence. They were completing their second year, had crowned their second class of World Champion Cowgirls, with fourteen-year-old Amy McGilvray out-pointing her older, more experienced peers for the All-Around title, and had elected a new slate of officers for 1950, headed by Nancy Binford as president.

Cathey and a few other journalists had begun writing articles about the GRA and some of its more prominent members. These were published in national magazines such as *Western Horseman, Hoofs & Horns,* and *Back in the Saddle.* Girls across the country read those articles and inquired about how they could join the GRA, or better yet, how they could get a GRA rodeo in their own town.

James Cathey photo–2015.006.9.23.9.8

With the 1950 season quickly approaching, the GRA officers decided they needed a headquarters office and someone to handle incoming mail and inquiries. During the first two years, president Margaret Owens Montgomery had managed those duties out of her home, in her "spare time."

James suggested they check into the place where he had established his office earlier in the year: Livestock Exchange Building, in the Fort Worth Stockyards area, right next to the arena where the Cowtown Rodeo was held and just a short drive from Will Rogers Memorial Coliseum, home of the Fort Worth Stock Show Rodeo. The GRA Board of Directors seized on the idea and soon became Cathey's next-door neighbor.

Vivian White riding saddle bronc at the 1949 Fort Smith All Girl Rodeo. Vivian was never bucked off while competing in her 15-year career.

Around this same time, incoming president Nancy Binford asked James to step in and take over as the GRA's first paid publicity director. "We can only pay $75 per month," she told him, "but the benefits of long hours, hard work, and endless travel, paid out of your own pocket should make you feel right at home. Besides, we really need your help."

Knowing this would be a major time commitment, James agreed to accept the position under two conditions. First, he requested that Margaret Owens Montgomery stay on the board in a role to support his efforts. He knew how much

James Cathey photo–2015.006.5.14.0.1

Girls Rodeo Association at the Fort Stockton All Girl Rodeo, May, 1950.

*Front cover of the
May 1950 issue of* Powder Puff and Spurs.

Historic document image courtesy of the National Cowboy & Western
Heritage Museum, Oklahoma City, Oklahoma

Margaret had contributed to PR efforts during her two years as president and that her continued participation would be essential to his success. Secondly, he would serve in that position for only one year because of the strain he knew it would place on his growing photography business.

Nancy replied, "It was Margaret's idea in the first place and she's already accepted the board position of publicity agent for next year."

A deal was struck, and history-making events were set in motion.

One of the first tasks James undertook was creating what Dixie Reger Mosley would refer to in a 2018 interview as "that little magazine he used to send out." Some people called it a pamphlet, others called it a newsletter, but Cathey called it "*Powder Puff and Spurs,* the only magazine in the world devoted exclusively to the Girls Rodeo Association."

Each issue of *PP&S,* or *The Powder Puff* as some people called it, was chock full of information about the GRA. It contained a list of all the officers and the directors responsible for each of the association's operating areas: calf roping; bareback; bull riding; cutting horse; optional roping; contract performers; and sponsor events. There were sections recognizing donors, advertisers, and other supporters; news about people and events from around the world of rodeo; personal updates about members near and far; highlights and results from recent rodeo events; and reminders of upcoming rodeos, with details about entry requirements and fees. In

addition, Cathey published stunning pictures of the girls
in action, portraits of GRA leaders and photos from award
presentations. Possibly its most important feature was an
active Letters to the Editor column, where readers could ask
questions, offer praise or criticism, and make suggestions for
improving the GRA.

Over the next two years, that "little magazine" became
a social lifeline for GRA members, keeping them in touch
with each other in an era when cell phones and computers
were not even a dream. It also became a pipeline for bringing
in new members, helping the GRA continue to enjoy rapid
growth.

PP&S was published monthly, even though James was
still traveling constantly, trying to make as many rodeos,
horse shows, and roping or cutting events as he possibly
could. He was also writing more than ever. In addition
to serving as editor and publisher of *PP&S*, James was
the publication's primary writer, and he was still writing
regular articles for several other industry publications and
newspaper press releases about GRA events.

Near the end of his year as publicity director, Cathey
wrote an article in *PP&S*, addressed to all GRA members,
recapping some of his accomplishments during the year:

- "First, the directors were taken to the offices of the *Fort
  Worth Star Telegram,* where they were photographed
  and interviewed. The paper followed up with a half
  dozen articles about the GRA because of the interest

generated. Also falling in line was the *Fort Worth Press* and two wire services, UP and AP, carrying news from Fort Worth to every newspaper in the nation.

- When officers were elected, arrangements were made to have them interviewed and televised by WBAP-TV.
- Valuable publicity was obtained and connections were made in Denver, at the National Rodeo Convention, which were very beneficial to the GRA.
- Made it a point to be on hand at all major GRA contests, helping get girls interviews with press and radio. At Colorado Springs, arranged interviews with the Denver Post sports editor, Marvin McCarthy, who ran a huge feature article on the sports page about the GRA.
- In Childress, arranged for a film crew from Universal Studios to show up and shoot a newsreel of the GRA rodeo which would be shown in movie theaters around the country and *Look* magazine was also on hand at my request.
- There were approximately thirty press releases mailed on each All Girl Rodeo which were published in practically every leading western magazine (plus some more) in the nation.
- Arranged for GRA advertising space, at no charge, in sixteen issues of *Rodeo News*.
- Compiled a complete publicity file, with photographic portraits, action photos, accomplishments and awards, for all GRA members.
- Prepared and printed a complete mailing list consisting of approximately 700 names of persons interested or who should be interested in GRA activities.
- Personally wrote approximately four dozen articles on members of the GRA that were published in newspapers and magazines, and supplied information and photos for other writers.

James Cathey photo–2015.006.6.17.0.12

LaTonne Sewalt on Little Joe leaves the third barrel of the cloverleaf for the homeward dash at the 1950 Jacksboro All Girl Rodeo.

Barrel racing was already a "ladies' event" in a few rodeos, judged mainly on style and reining skills–sometimes even on the appearance of the Sponsor Girls' clothing–before the GRA set standard distances for their three-barrel course and began judging the event based solely on time for completion of the cloverleaf pattern.

Riding ability became even more important for barrel racers as the speeds got faster and the skills of both riders and horses became more finely tuned. The modern, crowd-pleasing sport of barrel racing has changed little since the GRA set the standards and established it as one of their favorite events.

James Cathey photo–2015.006.10.12.9.2

Jackie Worthington's championship form, seen high above the arena of the 1949 GRA Finals Rodeo, Corpus Christi, Texas.

The most popular rough-stock event at the early GRA rodeos was the bareback bronc riding. Jackie was almost always in the money of this event and the bull riding.

Even in the 1940s there were a few women entering as competitors with men in saddle bronc riding, where they were allowed, but bareback was thought to be too rough and tough for women. Jackie Worthington and her friend Rae Beach made it look easy.

- Personally secured prizes or cash donations for GRA events from at least ten donors.
- Edited and published regular monthly issues of *Powder Puff and Spurs.*"

Shortly thereafter, James published the following notice in *Powder Puff and Spurs:*

"While serving as director of publicity for the GRA it was my good pleasure to have associated with some mighty nice people who were ever so helpful in putting the publicity on a national basis. I taxed their generosity very heavily at times, but they were always ready when called on. To list them would take a volume, but they represented the following: *Star-Telegram, Press,* AP, UP, Acme, *Caller-Times,*

Denver Post, Back-in-the-Saddle, Western Horseman, Quarter Horse News, Bit & Spur, Hoofs & Horns, Look, WBAP-TV and Radio, KFJZ, Movietone, Universal, Paramount and NBC… just to mention a few. Also, all announcers where there were girls' events. On behalf of the GRA, its members, officers and myself, thanks a million to all of you and the many others. —JJC"

In January of 1951, having completed his one-year commitment, Cathey resigned from his position as GRA publicity director.

It had been a wildly successful year, much more so than he had expected when the year began. The GRA had become known and respected throughout the United States and Canada as the driving force behind women's rodeo, and James had established procedures and the framework for a professional publicity department which his successors could utilize to continue building public awareness of the GRA and its ongoing activities.

Although moving on from the day-to-day responsibility of managing publicity, Cathey continued to support the GRA by photographing their events and writing magazine articles featuring the girls. He also served as editor and publisher of *Powder Puff and Spurs* for almost another year and a half.

It had been a wildly successful year, much more so than he had expected when the year began.

James Cathey photo–2015.006.9.28.1.24   James Cathey photo–2015.006.9.23.9.9   James Cathey photo–2015.006.7.22.0.6

They called themselves "girls."

They were daughters of the West,

Right: Rose Garrett at the 1950 Jacksboro All Girl Rodeo. Other cowgirls on this page are unidentified.

James Cathey photo–2015.006.6.17.0.9

James Cathey photo–2015.006.9.29.1.36

James Cathey photo–2015.006.5.14.0.3

Marie Morris at the 1950 Fort Stockton All Girl Rodeo.

lovers of challenge, and mothers of women's competitive role in the modern sport of rodeo.

James Cathey photo–2015.006.9.4.9.26

Jackie Worthington at the 1949 Woodward, Okla. Rodeo.

43

Rae Beach at the 1950 Corpus Christie All Girl Rodeo.

Jackie Worthington doing her wraps at the 1950 Coleman All Girl Rodeo.

In working the 1949 Lawton and Fort Smith All Girl Rodeos, James Cathey became aware of how much need there was for good publicity to help in growing the number of fans and members of the young Girls Rodeo Association.

That October, the GRA Finals Rodeo opened in Corpus Christi on a Wednesday, and by mid-day Sunday Cathey had made sure that news reporters, photographers and newsreel cameramen from all around were on the scene for interviews and action shots of the rodeo cowgirls.

On the right-hand page, fourteen-year-old Amy McGilvray poses for the news shots of her receiving the trophy saddle as the 1949 World Champion Cowgirl, with the 1948 World Champion, Margaret Owens Montgomery, at her side.

Soon Cathey was hired as the GRA's first professional publicity director.

Judy Hays roping at the 1950 Coleman All Girl Rodeo.

Unidentified barrel racer at the 1950 Fort Stockton All Girl Rodeo.

James Cathey photo–2015.006.5.14.0.62

GRA champion roper Blanche Altizer Smith heeling with an unidentified team roper in the 1950 Fort Stockton All Girl Rodeo.

While working as rodeo clown at the 1950 Coleman All Girl Rodeo, Tad Lucas strapped chaps over her clown costume for a saddle bronc ride.

James Cathey photo–2015.006.5.28.0.1

James Cathey photo–2015.006.10.21.0.33

1950 GRA World Champion All-Around Cowgirl, Jackie Worthington with her championship awards and sponsor gifts.

James Cathey photo–2015.006.5.14.0.29

The youngest barrel racer at the 1950 Fort Stockton All Girl Rodeo, 4-year old Ada Lee Quigg from Dryden, Texas, the niece of GRA champion Blanche Altizer Smith.

James Cathey photo—2015.006.4.6.0.6

Marie Morris at the 1950 Coleman All Girl Rodeo.

James Cathey photo—2015.006.9.23.9.10

Jackie Worthington, 1949 Fort Smith All Girl Rodeo.

James Cathey photo—2015.006.12.1.9.12

Margaret Owens Montgomery on Joe Brown, 1949 Angleton All Girl Rodeo.

James Cathey photo—2015.006.9.2.9.45

At the 1949 Woodward, Oklahoma Rodeo. left to right, Thena Mae Farr, Tommie Green, Hoyt Heffner, Nancy Binford, Jackie Worthington, and Nancy Bragg.

James Cathey photo—2015.006.11.8.1.22

Flag bearers in the Grand Entry of the 1951 Tulsa All Girl Rodeo, from left to right: Nancy Bragg, Lucyle Cowey, Rae Beach, and Tad Lucas.

Jackie Worthington making the turn at the 1948 Texas State Fair Rodeo in Dallas.

Rose Garrett at the 1950 Coleman All Girl Rodeo.

Unidentified cowgirl finishes her 7-second ride at the 1949 Lawton All Girl Rodeo.

LaTonne Sewalt (left) and Janelle McGilvray (right) lead the parade through downtown Jacksboro, Texas, for the 1950 Jacksboro All Girl Rodeo. Most of the people present were Texans, but no one seemed to notice that Janelle's Lone Star flag was mounted upside-down.

Wilma Standard (left) and Nancy Bragg (right) lead the grand entry at the 1950 Corpus Christi All Girl Rodeo.

June Probst at the 1949 Santa Rosa Round-Up, Vernon, Texas.

James Cathey photo–2015.006.9.5.9.18

Nancy Bragg tearing through the flag race at the 1949 Woodward, Oklahoma Rodeo. It was here that Nancy won her first trophy buckle, for fastest combined times in the flag and barrel races. Below: (left to right) G.K. Lewallen, Todd Whatley, Nancy Bragg, Red Wilmer, Shorty Matlock, and J.D. Holleyman.

James Cathey photo–2015.006.9.5.9.25

Dude Barton (header) and Thena Mae Farr (heeler) in team tie-down roping at the 1950 Childress All Girl Rodeo.

Unidentified cowgirl determined to ride with an injured ankle at the 1949 GRA Finals Rodeo at Corpus Christi, Texas.

Rodeo clowns, Nancy Bragg (left) and Mary Swenson relaxing at the 1950 Jacksboro All Girl Rodeo.

This impossible-looking riding position is being demonstrated by Nancy Bragg at the 1949 Amarillo Rodeo. It was her signature "Falling Tower," that few other trick riders could duplicate.

Manuelita Mitchell at the 1949 Colorado City Rodeo.

50

LaTonne Sewalt on Little Joe makes a very tight turn at the 1950 Childress All Girl Rodeo.

Thena Mae Farr at the 1949 Fort Smith All Girl Rodeo.

Rae Beach at the 1950 Coleman All Girl Rodeo.

In front of the bucking chutes at the 1949 GRA Finals Rodeo, Corpus Christi, Texas, (left to right) Margaret Owens Montgomery, Blanche Altizer Smith, Amy McGilvray, Jackie Worthington.

Talented roper Ruby Gobble between go-rounds at the 1950 Jacksboro All Girl Rodeo.

James Cathey photo–2015.006.6.17.0.15

Pee Wee knows what to do when Janelle McGilvray speaks into his ear at the 1950 Jacksboro All Girl Rodeo.

James Cathey photo–2015.006.5.28.0.17

Blanche Altizer Smith throwing her famous tight loop at the 1950 Coleman All Girl Rodeo.

James Cathey photo–2015.006.10.21.0.7

Tommie Green at the 1950 Tulsa All Girl Rodeo.

James Cathey photo–2015.006.9.22.9.4

Vivian White riding saddle bronc at the 1949 Fort Smith All Girl Rodeo.

James Cathey photo—2015.006.5.12.0.2

Elaine Bell at the 1950 Fort Stockton All Girl Rodeo.

James Cathey photo—2015.006.4.7.0.29

Dixie Toalson, 1950 Belton All Girl Rodeo.

James Cathey photo—2015.006.11.8.1.23

A few of the GRA stars at the 1951 Tulsa All Girl Rodeo. Down front, left to right, Jackie Worthington, Billye Burk Gamblin. Standing, left to right, Rae Beach, Sally Taylor, Tad Lucas, Margaret Owens Montgomery, Nancy Bragg, unidentified, Judy Hays, Rose Garrett.

53

James Cathey photo–2015.006.5.5.60

James Cathey gathered women of the GRA in the arena of the May, 1949 Santa Rosa Round-Up at Vernon, Texas. While this group is only a portion of the GRA members at the rodeo, many of the early GRA leaders who are featured in this book are included in this historic portrait.

Down front, left to right: Nancy Bragg, unidentified, Sissy Allen, Amy McGilvray, Jackie Worthington, Margaret Owens Montgomery, Blanche Altizer Smith. Standing, left to right: Dude Barton, Nancy Binford, Judy Hays, Blanche Beutler, Thena Mae Farr, Dixie Reger. Horseback, left to right: June Probst, Fannie Mae Cox, unidentified, Janelle McGilvray.

ost of the thirty-eight founding members of the GRA were ranch women. Born and raised around horses and cattle, they learned the rhythm of a horse's walk early, often preferring that to a cradle—riding in the front of the saddle or, in the case of Dude Barton, tied to the saddle. Many had their own horses at age two or three and before they ever attended school were helping with chores and working as important hands on the family ranch.

Soon came responsibilities for corralling young calves, roping, breaking colts, branding, and so on. They rode out alone to check on pregnant heifers, mend fences, and protect the land.

Ranch life bred early independence, self-reliance, fearlessness and immense confidence. Above all, it bred adaptability. These women who started the GRA and competed in its rodeos were tough, strong, dedicated, and knew how to get things done. They were also feminine, creative, artistic, and caring friends who loved to have a good time. The mixing and blending of all these traits made for a wonderful group of exceptional women.

Here are a few of those special ladies.

James Cathey photo–2015.006.Binford

Nancy Binford, Co-Producer of the 1947 Tri-State All Girl Rodeo and Co-Owner of Tri-State All Girl Rodeo, Inc.

Nancy Binford lived most of her life on the ten-thousand-acre Binford Ranch north of Wildorado, Texas, settled by her father, Gene Binford. Although he had graduated from the University of Michigan at Ann Arbor with a law degree, Gene preferred the outdoors and sports and passed those passions on to his daughters, Nancy and her older sister, Barbara. Along with Nancy's mother, Kate, he created the M Bar Ranch, where he bred and trained horses, raised cattle, and experimented with new methods to control erosion. Tennis courts, a golf course, and a polo field were added for the athletic family.

Horses were a way of life for the Binfords. Nancy was in the saddle before the age of three and never got off. Their beloved ranch was a family affair, and they reveled in being together for raucous fun as well as more serious ranch work. They shared responsibilities, often riding out together to check on cattle or mend fences, and the girls often accompanied their parents on the feed wagon on cold winter days.

In 1934, when Nancy was thirteen and Barbara was sixteen, Gene Binford died, and Kate took over the ranch and ran it with the help of her two daughters. Mornings, she packed the girls off to school on their horses and met them later to drive the pastures in her car, pointing out calves that needed to be roped or cut and colts that needed to be broken. They doctored animals that were sick, checked on traps and fences, and tended to heifers heavy with spring calves. M Bar added Quarter Horses, breeding, training, and showing them in halter and conformation events. Kate was an excellent trainer and manager, and Nancy an excellent student. Ranching was in her blood.

Nancy Binford was also a star high school athlete, excelling in basketball and participating in most every sport offered. Well known for her beauty as well as her horsemanship, she was chosen Sweetheart of the Will Rogers Range Riders of Amarillo in 1939, and for the next four years she traveled with them to horse shows, rodeos, and other events, such as the inauguration of Governor Beauford Jester in Austin. In this role, she also competed in sponsor girl events at rodeos, often winning, but more importantly creating a close circle of friends among the other girls in attendance.

Nancy enrolled in Texas Tech, majoring in physical education. She missed her horses, and at her mother's suggestion, she took one along. She became chairman of the Women's Riding Club and was an original member of the "ghost riders," who rode their horses around the field at football games. She honed her leadership skills as president of the Women's Recreation Association and the Women's Athletic Association. She was a striking beauty in evening dress or jeans, though she preferred the latter.

After graduation, she taught health and physical education at Lubbock Senior High School in 1943–44, returning to the ranch the following year to help her mother, as ranch hands were

James Cathey photo–2015.006.9.16.0.34

Nancy Binford closes on a calf at the 1950 Childress All Girl Rodeo.

scarce during World War II. She was home and never moved away again. She once summed up her feeling about the land as: "You don't really own the land, it's just loaned to you. I feel like if you don't take care of it, you can't keep it. It takes a little bit of work and a whole lot of love."[13]

In 1947, Nancy and her close friend, Thena Mae Farr, produced the first all-girl rodeo in Amarillo. They went on to

13 Renée M. Laegreid, "'Performers Prove Beauty and Rodeo Can be Mixed': The Return of the Cowgirl Queen," *Montana The Magazine of Western History,* Spring 2004, 44–55.

establish Tri-State All Girl Rodeo, Inc. (1948–53), producing all-girl rodeos in San Angelo, Seymour, Colorado Springs, and Amarillo, among other places. They were talented leaders and dedicated ranchers who created opportunities for other rodeo women.

After the second Amarillo Tri-State All Girl Rodeo in 1948, the American Quarter Horse Association honored Nancy by selecting her to exhibit in their Chicago cutting horse contest and to travel around promoting the organization. She later commented, "This was the most rewarding event in my rodeo career."[14]

A founding member and perennial supporter of the GRA, Nancy served as president in 1950, the same year she won the World Champion Cutting Horse title. She continued competing in rough stock events through 1953 and then turned her rodeo attention toward cutting horse contests. She was inducted into the National Cowgirl Hall of Fame in 1979, joining her mother, Kate, from the class of 1976.

James Cathey photo–2015.006.Farr

Thena Mae Farr, Co-Producer of the 1947 Tri-State All Girl Rodeo and Co-Owner of Tri-State All Girl Rodeo, Inc.

Thena Mae Farr, the youngest child of Lola and Tom Farr, grew up on the Farr Ranch near Seymour, Texas. Before the age of three she was riding her own horse and grew up dreaming of having a ranch of her own.

She began making her ranch dreams come true by becoming a sponsored rodeo rider before she was ten. As a teenager she had the reputation of being an all-around ranch girl with several horses and cattle in her personal care, and she owned her own herd while still in high school.

Thena Mae was a talented student and an outstanding all-around athlete, serving as class secretary and basketball captain in 1942–43, but it was her equestrian skills and outgoing personality that earned her greater honors in the community. As her acclaim grew, she was chosen to

14 Charlene Walker, "Not for Men Only," *Texas Techsan Magazine*, July/August 1972.

represent Seymour in the annual Horse Show and Rodeo at Fort Worth for 1940 and 1941. Her hometown appreciated the tall blonde's beauty as much as her horsemanship and selected her as Miss Seymour from 1940 to 1944. She enjoyed representing Seymour at horse shows and rodeos all over Texas and relished the opportunity to compete for prizes and honors in the sponsor events that combined beauty, athleticism, and equestrian skills.

She was a true ranch girl, genuine and straightforward. She always disliked phony people but loved children and animals, both wild and tame. Thena Mae enjoyed good food, reading, travel, and above all, a good time. She liked boating, fishing, hunting, football, basketball and all horse-related sports.

James Cathey photo–2015.006.7.21.0.5

Thena Mae Farr, "Miss Seymour, Texas," proving that there can be more to pretty sponsor girls and rodeo queens than meets the eye. Here she rides a bronc at the 1950 Corpus Christi All Girl Rodeo.

After graduating from Seymour High School in 1944, Thena Mae enrolled in Texas State College for Women but soon returned home to full-time ranching. However, she still had a burning desire to compete, and rodeo life just spoke to her. Being a sponsor girl had gotten her into the rodeo arena but not in the capacity she wanted. She dreamed of the day she would have the opportunity to compete in rough stock and roping contests.

Thena Mae's enthusiasm for rodeo competition, especially the rough stock events, led her and Nancy Binford to produce the first truly all-girl rodeo at Amarillo's Tri-State Fair in 1947. They incorporated their production company as Tri-State All Girl Rodeo, Inc. and for the next five years produced all-girl rodeos in several western states, providing women opportunities they had long lacked. Farr also continued her championship ways, competing and winning saddles, trailers, and prize money in cutting, bareback bronc riding, barrel racing, and flag racing.

She and Nancy Binford dissolved their company in 1953 and turned their attention to other ventures. No one stepped forward to fill their shoes and produce true all-girl rodeos, but their inspired leadership had opened new paths and changed the ground rules for rodeo women.

A founding member of the GRA, Thena Mae enhanced the sport of girls' rodeo with her commitment to and support of providing opportunities for GRA members. She served as GRA president in the event-packed year of 1951 and was recognized for her dedication to women's rodeo by the National Cowgirl Hall of Fame with induction in 1985.

James Cathey photo–2015.006.Montgomery

Margaret Owens Montgomery, founding president of the Girls Rodeo Association.

Margaret Owens Montgomery was

born into the Owens ranching dynasty to Tom and Ella Owens near Ozona, Texas, in 1922. As a baby Margaret was carried in the front of her father's saddle as he rode out to oversee the NH Ranch, and by the time she could walk, she was taking horses out on her own. She and her younger sister Sug developed into excellent ranch hands, and worked alongside their parents, raising sheep and Angus cattle, roping, branding, and breaking colts.

Margaret fell in love with this life and shortly after high school graduation was ranching on her own in nearby Rankin, riding the ranges and looking after her flocks. She also excelled in area rodeos as a sponsor girl, where her outstanding roping arm and cutting horse prowess won her not only acclaim but also trophy buckles and saddles.

In 1940, the Sheep and Goat Raisers Association chose

James Cathey photo–2015.006.10.16.9.3

Margaret Owens Montgomery riding bareback at the 1949 Corpus Christi GRA Finals Rodeo.

Margaret to represent them at Fort Worth's Southwestern Exposition and Fat Stock Show. She practiced roping with her well-known "Margaret determination" and won the sponsor contest, missing only two calves during the entire show. She also won a coveted invitation to the Madison Square Garden Rodeo that fall.

She attended TCU for a time, where she met her husband, Vic Montgomery, a star football player and a champion calf roper. They later divorced and Margaret returned to her maiden name and her ranching life in Rankin. All along, she continued in sponsor events, also competing in the separate girl's matched roping contests, which were often held in conjunction with RCA rodeos.

The West of the Pecos Rodeo was one of Margaret's favorites. It was there in 1945 that she scored her first real rodeo experience in the timed barrel race. She wanted more. In later years she won that rodeo's Girl's Calf Roping Championship four years in a row.

An insight into her comes from her sister Sug: "Margaret could be quiet and serious, but very cordial in a matter-of-fact way. Sometimes, she liked to kick back and have a good time with her friends, relaxing from a regimented time schedule of practices, taking care of horses or ranch business. She also enjoyed helping others hone their competitive skills. She was always strong and determined."

When talk of starting a girls' organization began in earnest at Amarillo's first Tri-State All Girl Rodeo in 1947, the cowgirls selected Margaret as their representative. She called the meeting for San Angelo; she and Sug arrived with

James Cathey photo–2015.006.9.25.1.31

Margaret with her favorite barrel and roping horse, Joe Brown.

61

the important legal documents for organizing in hand; and Margaret was elected as the first president of the Girls Rodeo Association. She was the dedicated leader the fledgling group needed, spending the two years of her presidency traveling all over the country at her own expense, explaining to people what the GRA was doing and engendering important support. Her parents and sister were also a great help to the early GRA.

In 1948, Margaret won the first GRA Championship in barrel racing (on Pee Wee, a horse she shared with Amy McGilvray) as well as the first Cutting Horse Championship and the GRA All-Around World Champion title.

For three years, Margaret attended every all-girl rodeo, often riding her registered Quarter Horse gelding, Joe Brown, to victory. She was the Wild Cow Milking Champion of 1949, and in her first four years as a GRA member she won thirteen buckles and five saddles. Her promising rodeo career was cut short in 1955 when she died in an auto accident.

Margaret was inducted into the National Cowgirl Hall of Fame in 1976.

James Cathey photo–2015.006.Barton

Dude Barton, founding vice president of the Girls Rodeo Association.

Mary Ellen "Dude" Barton, the youngest of Wilbur and Ella's nine children, grew up on the Cross 6 Ranch on the North Pease River east of Flomot, Texas. When she was just a baby, she cried to go with her dad to the fields. He would put her on an old plow horse, where she would ride until she fell asleep. When lifting her off caused her to awaken and cry, she would go right back on. By the age of two she was riding behind her father on his fastest cutting horse, "hanging on like a flea," while he worked cattle. Still so small that she had to be tied in the saddle so she wouldn't fall off, Dude helped drive cattle from Flomot to Matador.

Dude's relatives recall the spunk that earned her that name. According to family lore, when she was small Old Jim was her mount. Usually reliable with the youngest riders, one day Old Jim couldn't resist running when the other horses ran, causing Dude to fall off. When she came crying to the house, someone asked, "Where'd you hit?" The four-year-old's response was fiery, "I hit on the ground, where the hell you think I hit."[15]

On the ranch, everyone worked. The boys and girls each had a mule team that he or she was responsible for working, feeding, harnessing and caring for. The children learned to ride horses and work cattle early. Ranch chores of riding, roping, and branding were a welcome relief from farming with cranky old mules.

During the school year they lived in Matador. Dude loved playing basketball and was elected football sweetheart, but the rodeos were where her heart really was. At fifteen she entered her first rodeo competition at Matador during Shannon Davidson Day. This event honored Flomot's native son, who was the victor in a Pony Express contest sponsored by the Nocona Boot Company.[16]

James Cathey photo–2015.006.6.15.0.15

Dude Barton on Betty Barton running the barrels at the 1950 Jacksboro All Girl Rodeo. Her horsemanship skills helped her excel at racing, cutting and roping events.

15 "Mary Ellen 'Dude' Barton," *Motley County Tribune*, 17 Mar. 1988, 1 and 9.
16 "Flomot Woman Featured in Amarillo News Story," *Motley County Tribune*, 6 Feb. 2003, 5.

The following year, 1940, she won her first saddle in a sponsor contest and just kept on winning. She also competed in matched events when the opportunity came, topping Sydna Yokley in roping and out-dueling Fern Sawyer in a cutting horse event. Dude rode in Fay Kirkwood's last rodeo in Wichita Falls in 1942 and won virtually everything. The story was that the only reason she didn't bring home Sheppard Air Force Base was because Kirkwood didn't offer it as a prize. That same year she bested fifty-six men in a ribbon racing contest.

Dude was one of the stars of the 1947 Tri-State All Girl Rodeo in Amarillo, where she won both the sponsor and calf roping contests. At Midland that same year she became the first contestant ever to take home both the $1,500 saddle for the sponsor contest and the $600 trailer in the cowgirls cutting horse contest. "It was a two-horse trailer, and all I had was an old open-top trailer," Barton said with a grin. "I thought I'd sure gone uptown when I won that Hobbs horse trailer."[17]

She went on to help organize the Girls Rodeo Association as both a founding member and the first GRA Vice President.

Dude's favorite rodeo events were calf and team roping, barrel and flag racing, and the cutting competition. Roping came naturally to her—from years of experience on the ranch. As she once described it, catching in the arena was a matter of winning or losing for the rodeo roper, but if she missed in the pasture, she still had to go after the calf or steer until she caught it. Catching the calf the first time was better all around for her, in the pasture or the arena.

She was a great competitor and also a great friend with a mischievous sense of humor. When you were around Dude, you had fun. She entered GRA rodeos up through the 1953 Colorado Springs contest, although ranching responsibilities

James Cathey photo–2015.006.6.15.0.21

Dude Barton wrapping three legs at the 1950 Jacksboro All Girl Rodeo.

17 Ibid.

claimed an increasing portion of her time, and she retired from the professional circuit after that, returning to her ranch life.

As the other early GRA members, Dude formed deep and lasting friendships, which she cherishes to this day.

Mary Ellen "Dude" Barton was inducted into the National Cowgirl Hall of Fame in 1984.

Jackie Worthington, first general director of individual Girls Rodeo Association events.

Jackie Worthington was a real pistol. She was only four feet, eight inches tall and weighed barely one hundred pounds. Betty Dusek once commented, "she wasn't as big as a bar of soap, but that girl could ride anything." As small as she was, Jackie still packed a wallop and feared no Brahma bull or bucking horse.

On her way to the 1947 Tri-State Rodeo in Amarillo, she stopped by Paducah to pick up a friend, landing her Cessna in a field of sunflowers so tall they came all the way up to the cockpit windows. That caught her attention and she vowed to never do anything that risky again. But nothing could shake Jackie's determination when it came to rodeo competition. She went on to win first place in both bareback bronc and bull riding that weekend.

Jackie was known for her kindness and generosity as well as her fierce competitive spirit. At one rodeo ceremony, when awarded a palomino horse for first place, she turned to Thena Mae Farr, the second place winner, and gifted her the horse—whereupon Thena Mae gifted her new boots to Jackie.

The same consideration extended to her ranch life. Once a visitor, seeing two old horses standing around in the pasture near her house, asked Jackie why she didn't put them down. A broad smile slowly spread across her face as she looked at the old work horses, now nearing their end, "I would never do that. They gave me their whole lives, helping with the ranch, and here is where they will stay."

She and her sisters Mary and Ada grew up on the West Fork Ranch near Jacksboro, Texas, working as ranch hands alongside their father L.A. and absorbing his love of the land and his commitment to that land. As his prime ranch hands, they learned to rope, break colts, brand and dehorn cattle—in short, they did it all. L.A. was a big supporter of his daughters' rodeo ambitions, teaching them, coaching them, and creating performance opportunities for them in the West Fork Rodeos, starting in 1944. Jackie even gave twice-daily exhibitions of bull riding and bareback bronc riding one year.

After completing high school in 1942, Jackie attended Texas State College for Women in Denton, graduating with a degree in physical education and recreation. She also studied animal husbandry. In 1947, while rodeoing almost every weekend, she attended North Texas State College to earn her master's degree.

Jackie was multi-talented. A licensed pilot, she flew to many rodeos and to visit friends—usually alone. She was also an accomplished musician, who played the piano for many local civic groups. She filmed amateur movies and entertained her cowgirl friends with showings of their rodeo antics. She loved to have a good time and was known to party with the best of them after a rodeo.

A founding member of the GRA, Jackie became the first general chairman of individual event directors and the director of bareback riding. She continued her strong support of the organization as director for many years and as president in 1954–56.

In her fifteen years of rodeoing, Jackie won twenty-three world championships including all-around, bull riding, bareback bronc riding, ribbon roping, and cutting. When the National Cowgirl Hall of Fame opened in 1975, she was justly honored as a member of the first inductee class.

James Cathey photo—2015.006.12.1.9.7

James Cathey photo—2015.006.11.11.1.10

Jackie Worthington won 23 world championships in her 15 years of rodeoing with the GRA. Above, she rides a bull at the 1949 Angleton All Girl Rodeo. Right, she is presented with yet another trophy buckle at the 1951 Tulsa All Girl Rodeo by RCA champion, Jim Shoulders.

67

James Cathey photo–2015.006.D.Reger

Dixie Reger, first director of contract acts and the official Girls Rodeo Association clown from 1948 to 1953.

Dixie Reger was born into a rodeo entertainment family. Her father, Monte, had discovered and trained a longhorn steer with unusually long and twisted horns and they traveled the country exhibiting Bobby. Soon they were part of the Jim Eskew Wild West Show and Rodeo, and Monte was often both announcer and performer on Bobby, riding him and jumping him over convertibles.

Fearless, Dixie debuted as a trick rider at the age of five on her thirty-six-inch Shetland pony Tom Thumb. Her older sister Virginia also performed as a trick rider and roper, and Buddy, her brother, was a rodeo clown. The Reger children were breadwinners and had to be ready to perform and look good doing so. That meant no activities where they might sprain an ankle or break a bone or incur an unsightly sunburn. In addition to grooming and caring for their mounts, Virginia, Buddy, and Dixie were responsible for ensuring that their elaborate costumes were clean, in good repair and ready for each performance. They practiced to perfection, and the crowds loved them—especially tiny Dixie.

After leaving the Eskew show, the Regers performed for other producers, and Monte expanded his rodeo announcing career. He was the announcer for Fay Kirkwood's Wichita Falls All Girl Rodeo in 1942, and when they needed a clown, promptly responded, "Dixie can do it." And so, eleven-year-old Dixie added to her repertoire, borrowing Buddy's costume and face paint and launching her rodeo clown career.

The family had a ranch near Woodward, Oklahoma, where they returned periodically to prepare for their next trip. Monte, who loved horses, raised Palominos and Quarter Horses. Dixie learned the skills of a ranch hand. She especially enjoyed roping. She also left the curriculum of the Calvert Correspondence School behind and enrolled in Woodward High School, where she tasted a regular school experience, although she usually arrived a month late in the fall and had to leave early in the spring to accommodate the rodeo year. She graduated at sixteen and promptly began showing Quarter Horses—and winning.

When the call came for entrants in Nancy Binford and Thena Mae Farr's 1947 All Girl Rodeo at Amarillo's Tri-State Fair, Dixie Reger was ready. This would be her first competitive rodeo experience and she entered every event: bronc, bull and trick riding, calf and ribbon roping, barrel racing and the wild Brahma scramble—and she clowned the entire show. She was sore but happy, and she discovered she absolutely loved roping.

A founding member of the Girls Rodeo Association, Dixie was elected to their board as the first director of contract acts and later served multiple terms as vice president. She put her heart and soul into helping the GRA succeed, entering every rodeo she could possibly manage. As she put it: "If we had a rodeo, I was there." Most of the girls felt the same way. The girls were always willing to help one another, to loan you a rope or their horse, but in the arena they competed to win. Thinking of her good friend Ruby Gobble: "I wanted to beat her as bad as she wanted to beat me."

Dixie dove into rodeoing—until the 1953 Colorado Springs rodeo was over. Sitting around afterwards, she announced that she was retiring and getting married. And she did.

In reflecting on her rodeo years and the friendships that still endure from those days, she remarks: "You meet some

James Cathey photos, from top, 2015.006.4.7.0.36, 2015.006.4.7.0.27, and 2015.006.9.28.1.13

Dixie Reger still reigns as one of the most enthusiastic rodeo cowgirls of all time. She participated as a contestant in almost every event while she worked as the rodeo clown for the all-girl rodeos, and she and her sister, Virginia, preformed trick riding and roping. The top two photos are from the 1950 Belton All Girl Rodeo, and the one below is from the 1951 San Antonio All Girl Rodeo.

wonderful, wonderful people." Dixie still attends almost every annual National Cowgirl Hall of Fame luncheon and looks forward to reminiscing with friends from her rodeo days.

Dixie was inducted into the National Cowgirl Hall of Fame in 1982 and into the National Cowboy & Western Heritage Museum's Rodeo Hall of Fame in 2003. She was also selected as the recipient of the American Cowboy Culture Award for Pioneer Women at the Cowboy Symposium in Lubbock in 2004.

James Cathey photo–2015.006.Lucas

Tad Barnes Lucas in one of her trick riding outfits, probably in 1950.

Barbara Inez "Tad" Barnes was born in 1902 on a ranch outside Cody, Nebraska. Lorenzo Barnes brought his family to Nebraska in an oxcart when it was still Indian territory, and he was the first white settler. Their youngest child, Barbara, was born there. Because she never learned to crawl, just slithered along on her back, the family nicknamed her Tadpole, and soon she was just Tad.

Her father ran a general store on the edge of the Sioux reservation, raised and traded horses, and ran the ranch. Tad and her siblings were the ranch hands. She rode horses from the time she can remember, and by seven, she was breaking colts and riding calves as well as harnessing her team, plowing and raking the hay fields with her brothers and sisters. For recreation they challenged other ranch children as well as the Indian children to horseback races, steer riding, and other contests. Tad also hung around the store and watched as Lorenzo, a kind and generous man, helped his customers when times were tight. She inherited his gregarious but gentle nature and his happy disposition.

During World War I, Tad rode bulls and broncs down the main streets of Cody to raise money for the Red Cross. At fifteen, she made her professional debut in a steer riding competition against Mildred Douglas at the Nebraska State Fair and won $25. "Well," she said, "that ruined me, right

James Cathey photo–2015.006.6.17.0.5

Tad Lucas having great fun riding saddle bronc at the 1950 Jacksboro All Girl Rodeo.

there." She soon moved to Fort Worth with one of her brothers, continued competing in local rodeos and joined California Frank Hafley's Wild West Show, where she fell in love with trick riding. The show went to Mexico, then traveled around the United States, where she met her future husband, Buck Lucas. She gained renown as a saddle bronc rider and a relay racer, and in 1924, she and Buck were invited to join Tex Austin's London Rodeo in Wembley Stadium. There, Tad made her first professional trick ride and wowed the crowds.

At that time, trick riding was a competitive rodeo event. Riders continually invented new tricks, adding increasing difficulty to stay on top. Tad created the back drag, considered one of the most demanding tricks—hanging off the back of her favorite horse, Candy Lamb, arms outstretched and hair dragging the arena ground. This became her signature trick.

When the couple returned from London, Tad's rodeoing career took off even more. They returned to Fort Worth and built an arena behind their home where Tad trained, but they were often on the road. She performed in Madison Square Garden for several years, retiring the famous $10,000 MGM Silver Trophy for winning Champion All-Around Cowgirl at the Garden, three years in a row (1928–30). She continued to perform to increasing acclaim throughout the 1930s and 1940s. Trick riding had moved from a competitive event to an exhibition in the 1930s, and Tad was still in high demand for the major rodeos, even when women's events began to fall by the wayside.

James Cathey photo–2015.006.10.13.9.39

Tad Lucas enters the arena in her debut as a clown at the 1949 Corpus Christi GRA Finals Rodeo.

71

This tiny five-foot, one-inch cowgirl, with the big talent and the broad, beaming smile became known as the First Lady of Rodeo. When the GRA was formed in 1948, she was there in San Angelo along with her daughter and sometimes trick riding partner Mitzi Lucas Riley. Tad's status and support brought publicity and authenticity to the fledgling organization. She was always generous with her time and effort and especially encouraging to the younger girls.

Tad performed in GRA rodeos as a saddle bronc and trick rider for several years, but it was as a clown in red wig and red polka dot costume, teamed with Dixie Reger, that she really shone.

Tad was the first woman inducted into the National Cowboy & Western Heritage Museum's Rodeo Hall of Fame (1967). She entered the National Cowgirl Hall of Fame in 1978 and was honored by the ProRodeo Hall of Fame in 1979.

James Cathey photo–2015.006.Sawyer

Fern Sawyer, All-Around Champion at the historic 1947 Amarillo All Girl Rodeo.

Fern Sawyer, born on a ranch near Yeso, New Mexico, was put on a horse at the age of one, and was never far from horses for the rest of her life. In her words: "I was on a horse from morning till night, growing up. Daddy always told me, 'You don't have to ride. You can either help me, or you can go help your mother in the house. That's your choice. But if you go with us, you are going to be treated just like one of the cowboys. You don't quit. You are just one of them.'"[18] She chose the outside and rode beside her father on their Crossroads Ranch near present-day Tatum, New Mexico, roping, branding, and working the land.

No school bus came near the ranch, so Fern lived with her paternal grandparents and enrolled in the Brownfield, Texas, schools, also studying piano and helping with the teas

18 Teresa Jordan, *Cowgirls: Women of the American West, An Oral History* (Garden City: Anchor Press/Doubleday, 1982), 229.

72

and other social events her grandmother gave. Whenever possible, she returned to the ranch and learned the cattle business at her father's knee. He taught her well, and she became known for wanting things "done right."

Fern began her rodeo career at fifteen as a sponsor girl in Lovington, New Mexico, running barrels and competing as often as possible. She was invited to the Madison Square Garden rodeo several times and won the All-Around World Champion Cowgirl title in 1938. She also frequently competed in matched roping and cutting horse competitions throughout the 1930s and 1940s.

Fern played to win. She once came in second to Barry Hart on his famous cutting horse Berlin at a Texas rodeo in 1941. Later she heard him say he would sell his horse for $1,000, and she asked her father to buy Berlin. He was horrified, but Fern's mother, Dessie, stepped in, and the deal was struck. It was World War II. Fern immediately renamed him Belen, and he was, she maintained, the meanest horse she ever knew, but also the best. She won many cutting matches on Belen, and in a 1943 charity event in Tatum, New Mexico, became the only female to ever beat legendary cutting champion Bob Crosby. Stunned, Crosby wanted a rematch but was killed in a tragic Jeep accident before it could be held.[19]

Fern kept competing and kept winning, and in 1945, as the only woman allowed to enter the national cutting horse contest in Fort Worth, she beat out 150 men to become the Cutting Horse World Champion. She was also a founder of the National Cutting Horse Association and became the only woman elected to its Hall of Fame in 1985.

A true pioneer for women on the professional rodeo circuit, Fern threw herself into rodeoing: tag races, barrel racing, calf roping, team roping, bronc riding, bull riding, and cutting events. You were either her friend and could do no

Photographer unknown. Image courtesy the National Cowgirl Museum and Hall of Fame, Fort Worth, Texas.

Fern Sawyer shows amazing balance and cool determination while bull riding at an all-girl rodeo. The exact event and date are unknown, but Fern may have been rodeo's best dressed bull rider of the year.

19 Ibid., 227–235.

wrong or her enemy. And the girls of the GRA were definitely her friends. She would do—and did—anything for them. At Nancy Binford and Thena Mae Farr's 1947 Amarillo All Girl Rodeo, she competed in multiple events, but when too few cowgirls entered bull riding to make it a competition, she volunteered to ride as part of an exhibition. Her father was very much against her riding, but told her, "If you're going to get on that bull you'd better ride him to the end." She rode the entire eight seconds, her hand so tightly clenched she broke it in nine places. The $7 she made in mount money paled beside the $1,000 plus it cost her father to piece her hand back together. But in that very first competitive all-girl rodeo, Fern was crowned the All-Around Girls Rodeo Champion.

A charter member of the GRA, she was elected its first director of cutting horse events in 1948. In May of that year, life changed forever for the New Mexico cowgirl when oil was discovered on the Sawyer family's Crossroads Ranch. Before the well was even tested, they knew, and invited 700 of their closest friends to a celebratory barbecue tabled with 1,500 pounds of prime meat.

Known as "Salty Fern Sawyer" for her liberal use of four-letter words, she inherited her mother's sense of style and was a flashy and flamboyant dresser. Whether in boots or heels, Fern lit up any venue she entered. She worked hard, played hard, and never gave in.

Fern's motto was "do as much as you can as fast as you can for as long as you can." She lived that motto. It was after a good ride while visiting friends near Blanco, Texas, that she dismounted her horse, suffered a fatal heart attack and slipped away—with her boots on.

She was inducted into the National Cowgirl Hall of Fame in 1976 and the National Cowboy & Western Heritage Museum's Rodeo Hall of Fame in 1991.

James Cathey photo–2015.006.10.12.9.31

Blanche Altizer Smith, roping at the 1949 GRA Finals Rodeo, Corpus Christi, Texas.

Blanche Altizer Smith.

Bull rider Bud Smith loved his bulls and his bull riding more than anything in rodeo—until he met calf roper Blanche Altizer. She loved him, but told him that she wouldn't marry a bull rider. "If you want to marry me, you're gonna have to learn to rope," she said.[20] So he did. They tied the knot soon after, and for the next forty-seven years the couple continued to rope together.

Blanche grew up in South Texas on the Altizer family's sheep ranch near Del Rio, with her older sister Ora and younger brother Jim Bob, all three outstanding rodeo competitors. Like most ranch children, Blanche learned to ride almost before she learned to walk, and horses were always a part of her life. She was a top hand on her father's ranch, especially in roping and breaking yearlings, working alongside her father and brother.

As a teenager, Blanche was a star softball player in the days of the fast pitch, and had she chosen to do so, she could have starred in almost any form of girls' athletics. It was said that with her strong roping arm, she was probably too much for most of the male heroes in arm wrestling as well. She was a multi-talented athlete with an A-plus personality. Vivacious and popular, she participated in many school activities, including playing in the orchestra and acting a leading role in her high school senior play *(Youth Takes Over)*. A formal graduation dance was also given in her honor at the Del Rio Country Club that year.

After the versatile Blanche captured a robber in 1944, she became Del Rio's Honorary Chief of Police. And as if that weren't enough, she was also a model, an accomplished

James Cathey photo–2015.006.Altizer

Blanche Altizer Smith, first GRA team tying and cow milking director.

---

20 *Del Rio News Herald*, 12 Sep. 2002.

James Cathey photo–2015.006.9.16.0.7

Blanche Altizer Smith, 1950 GRA
Champion Calf roper, at the Childress All
Girl Rodeo of that same year.

stenographer, made most of her own clothes, liked to cook, enjoyed dancing, and delighted in wearing pretty clothes when she competed in rodeos.

But ranching was simply in Blanche Altizer's blood. Although she was an honor student throughout her school days, graduating from high school with a 94 average, she chose ranching over college and reveled in caring for the land and watching over the cattle and sheep and horses. While still in high school, she had begun participating as a sponsor girl in rodeos all over the area and continued winning in the barrel racing and roping competitions that spread in the mid-1940s. She was energetic and highly competitive and rarely missed an opportunity to test her skills. Among her favorite contests were the West of the Pecos Rodeo, the Midland Rodeo and, of course, Del Rio's rodeo, where she competed on her favorite mare, Betty, in calf roping, team tying and barrel racing.

Blanche competed in the first competitive All Girl Rodeo in Amarillo, finishing high in team tying and barrel racing and placing in several daily events. The all-girl rodeos that followed gave her the opportunity she had longed for and she went on to rodeo for years, adding to her collection of buckles and saddles. She was a true rodeo promoter. Although a champion herself, she always had time for the younger cowgirls with words of encouragement and hints that helped. She accepted the cheers, the accolades and the awards in stride. The famous Altizer smile—and her two feet always solidly on the ground—greeted those who came to congratulate her, and she was quick to congratulate her winning peers as well.[21]

In addition to her competitive vein, Blanche was quite a writer, as shown by her excellent article on the Girls Rodeo Association in the July,1953, issue of *Western Horseman*.

A founding member of the GRA, Blanche served as their first team tying and cow milking director, an event director for several years, and secretary from 1955 to 1958. She was their champion calf roper and champion team roper in 1950.

Blanche was honored with induction into both the National Cowgirl Hall of Fame (1976) and the Texas Rodeo Hall of Fame (2014).

She was truly the pride of South Texas.

James Cathey photo—2015.006.10.12.90.43

Wanda Harper Bush in the Wild Cow Milking event at the 1950 Corpus Christi All Girl Rodeo.

Wanda Harper Bush grew up roping and tying goats to help her father, famed roper Alvin Harper, on their ranch near Mason, Texas. She followed in his footsteps as a rodeo champion and became the most decorated cowgirl in the history of the Girls Rodeo Association, winning a total of thirty-two world championships in all-around, calf roping, ribbon roping, cutting, barrel racing, and flag racing.

When her father realized that his petite five foot, one inch daughter had her heart set on rodeoing, he built a practice arena and began coaching her. One evening they were working on her roping skills, and he promised to keep releasing calves until she missed one. Finally, exhausted, he gave up and went back to the house.

When she left home to rodeo, her father's advice was simply: "Now honey, when you go out in the world you are going to be thrown with all kinds of people. You'll be with the rich and the poor, the good and the bad, but you just be

James Cathey photo—2015.006.Harper

Wanda Harper Bush, a GRA charter member at age 16, went on to become the most decorated cowgirl in GRA history, with thirty-two championships.

---

21 "Mrs. Smith honored with buckle, party," *Del Rio News Herald*, 19 Jun. 84, 7.

James Cathey photo–2015.006.10.16.9.11

Wanda Harper Bush turning it on at the 1949 GRA Finals Rodeo in Corpus Christi, Texas.

James Cathey photo–2015.006.10.12.90.43

Wanda Harper Bush finishes her tie down 1950 Fort Stockton All Girl Rodeo.

Wanda and always remain yourself and you'll do all right." And she did. She was both talented and determined.

Journalist Willard Porter recounted a legendary story of her inventiveness from an all-girl roping contest in Laramie, Wyoming: "One of Wanda's 'draws' was a fast-running critter which went all the way to the end of the arena before the plucky little roper had a chance for a throw. She finally made a neat catch, but the pesky calf, foiled in his dash for freedom plunged through a small hole in the fence. So there were horse and calf joined by a stout rope, with a wire fence separating them.

One moment Wanda was on her horse, sizing up the situation. The next moment she was running down the rope and tying the calf. Some say Wanda went under the fence: others say she went over. Still others, and I'm inclined to agree with these latter observers, say that "She just went plumb through that blamed fence somehow!"[22]

It was said that she was "blessed with more talent in her little finger than most people ever acquire in a lifetime." This outstanding horsewoman joined the National Cowgirl Hall of Fame in 1978, the National Cowboy & Western Heritage Museum's Rodeo Hall of Fame in 2001 and the ProRodeo Hall of Fame in 2017

---

22 Willard Porter, "Wanda's Some Cowgirl..." *Hoofs and Horns*, August 1953.

78

James Cathey photo–2015.006.10.16.9.17

Betty Dusek finishing a wrap at the 1950 Corpus Christi All Girl Rodeo.

Betty Barron Dusek. When John and Ruby Barron went riding, they carried little two-year-old Betty with them in front of their saddles. She fell in love with horses and has never strayed. She still jokes that someone should create a perfume with the scent of horse.

As a young girl, Betty loved to ride and rope, and she skipped school whenever stock was being worked. Her father built an arena for Betty to practice roping their Spanish goats, and after school, she grabbed her rope, hit the arena and roped and roped and roped. She spent her summers practicing as well and soon graduated to calves.[23]

During World War II, a soldier's rodeo came to San Angelo, near her home in Van Court, Texas. Betty went and immediately knew that participating in rodeo was what she wanted to do in life. She redoubled her practice efforts. Her discipline and determination paid off when she was sixteen and entered a rodeo where the prize was the pick of eleven fillies. Her father teased that if she won, he would walk the horse home. She won—but didn't hold her father to his promise![24]

Betty competed in the famous 1947 Tri-State All Girl Rodeo in Amarillo. The following February found her in San Angelo as a founding member of the Girls Rodeo Association, where she was elected the GRA's first director of calf roping. In both 1948 and 1949 she won the GRA world championship in calf roping.

Betty was a consummate professional in the rodeo arena—a focused competitor, who knew how to win. She was also a great friend. She and Wanda Harper often traveled together to GRA rodeos. Betty recounts how, when she was pregnant with her first son, Wanda's horse was hurt and she

James Cathey photo–2015.006.Barron

Betty Barron Dusek, first GRA director of calf roping, won her last trophy saddle at the age of seventy-four.

23 Interview, March 16, 2018.
24 *San Angelo Standard-Times*, Interview, 25 Sep. 2010.

borrowed Betty's horse. Wanda promptly won with Betty loudly cheering her on.

Betty earned the respect of her peers for her dedication to rodeo. The verdict is "she shaped the sport of rodeo."

In 2010, the National Cowgirl Hall of Fame honored her commitment to rodeo by selecting her as an inductee, and later that same year the Texas Rodeo Hall of Fame inducted her as well.

James Cathey photo–2015.006.Beach

Rae Beach, trick rider, trick roper, calf roper, cow cutter, GRA bull rider and champion bareback bronc rider.

R ae Beach, eight-time GRA world champion bareback rider, couldn't remember a time when she wasn't around horses. She grew up on a ranch east of Los Angeles, California, where her father kept a string of horses and her earliest memories include being on horseback. As a ranch hand, she did it all.

That probably included playing on the backs of horses, since she became a trick rider as well as a trick roper. She was one of the equestrians who mastered the dangerous and exciting Roman standing race: where one foot is on the back of two different horses as they tear down the field. Rae's favorite trick!

Rae was simply fearless. She competed in bareback bronc and Brahma bull riding at the Amarillo Tri-State All Girl Rodeo in 1947, placing second to Jackie Worthington in the bareback competition. Although Rae moved to Texas in 1949, she often returned to California for the Los Angeles Sheriff's Championship Rodeo where she performed with her long-time trick-riding friends, thrilling audiences who knew her from the past. She also continued trick riding in Texas rodeos.

Rae was the GRA bronc riding director from 1951–1954 and won her first bareback championship in 1951. She loved the rough stock events but also excelled in calf roping and cutting.

James Cathey photo–2015.006.5.13.0.4

One of the GRA's best bareback bronc riders, Rae Beach, making it look easy at the 1950 Fort Stockton All Girl Rodeo.

She moved to the north side of Fort Worth, and when she wasn't on the road competing, she worked for years for Leddy's and Ryon's western stores. The story is that many Leddy's customers thought so highly of Rae, that when she was busy they would just wait around for her to be freed up to help them. People were just drawn to her.

James Cathey told the story of how Rae walked into the coffee shop at the Corpus Christi rodeo headquarters White Plaza Hotel. She let go with her "famous yell," and the whole place just came alive.

A striking beauty, Rae was asked during a 1951 interview if romance rode along the rodeo trail. "Not for me," she smiled. "I'll take the horses, they're easier to get along with."

81

James Cathey photo–2015.006.Gobble

Ruby Gobble, a rare female catch-loop roping artist.

Ruby Gobble, the "glamor girl of rodeo," grew up on the Gobble family ranch near Wickenburg, Arizona. The youngest of Myrtle and B. Gobble's five children, Ruby began riding desert burros at the age of three and soon could ride a horse and milk a cow. She also learned to play the ukulele at a young age and loved to entertain the family by performing western songs. Ruby's magnetic personality and gentle nature drew all kinds of ranch animals to her side. She was also a Wickenburg hometown favorite. Ruby was first known as a trick rider. By the age of twelve, she had broken and trained her trick-riding horse, Tony, and they performed at rodeos all across Arizona.

By the time she was crowned Queen of the Glendale, Arizona, World's Championship Rodeo in 1949, Ruby was performing with her Palomino horse, Taffy. But it was roping that stole her heart. She said, "When I started roping, I forgot my trick horses. I just loved it. I've always been a competitor."

Ruby launched her professional career at the 1950 Pikes Peak or Bust Rodeo in Colorado Springs, where she won first place in calf roping. The next year she joined the GRA, formed deep and lasting friendships and followed the rodeo circuit for several years, winning awards and world championships in both team and ribbon roping.[25] She was one of the few female catch-loop roping artists (throwing the slack over the horse's head).

Ruby often traveled to GRA rodeos with Nancy Binford, Nancy Bragg and Jackie Worthington. "There weren't many motels available in those days," she recalled. "One of us would get a room, and the other girls would bunk in the same room. The first one there got the bed, and the others had to sleep on the floor. We stayed in some real doozies!"

Between rodeos and in the off-season, Ruby worked for many years on the Binford ranch. "Nancy's mother, Katie,

25 Mary Lynn Roper, *KOAT - TV*, Evening News Tribute To Ruby by General Manager. Broadcast June 16, 2013. http://www.koat.com/article/rubby-gobble/4397664

James Cathey photo–2015.006.Goble.C.6.17.0.6

Ruby Gobble, champion roper, mounted near the back stock pens at the 1950 Jacksboro All Girl Rodeo.

was a stern taskmaster, and she worked our tails off, but I loved that woman to death," she stated.

In recognition of her outstanding roping talents and many contributions to ranching and women's rodeo, Ruby was inducted into the National Cowgirl Hall of Fame in 1982.

Other Notable Contributors

All-girl rodeos were popular events for spectators, but even more so for the cowgirls, who now had opportunities for competition that pre-WWII ranch women could only dream about. The 60 events of 1948 increased dramatically the following year, and the number of GRA members increased dramatically as well. By 1950 scores of women were regularly competing in all-girl rodeos and in RCA women's events sanctioned by the GRA. More than one hundred participants actually followed the GRA rodeo circuit on a regular basis. Many others did not travel from rodeo to rodeo, but eagerly entered rodeos close to their homes and ranches. Whether winning once, frequently peppering the winners lists, or just enjoying the experience of participating, these women relished the chance to test their skills against their peers and proudly wore their buckles and jackets to celebrations for the remainder of their lives.

In addition to those already profiled, other notable GRA contributors were:

- rough stock competitors – Jeannette Campbell, Lucyle Cowey, Jackie Flowers, Cookie Foster, Rose Garrett, Tommie Green, June Probst, Frances Weeg and Vivian White;
- calf ropers – Judy Hays, Margie Stuart, Sally Taylor and Isora Young;
- trick riders – Faye Blessing, Nancy Bragg, Jerry Ann Portwood Taylor, Mitzi Lucas Riley, Wilma Standard and Dixie Toalson;
- barrel racers – Amy McGilvray, Janelle McGilvray and LaTonne Sewalt;

while Billye Burk Gamblin, president in 1952–53; Fannie Mae Cox, association secretary; and Manuelita Mitchell, founding member and tireless GRA ambassador, contributed significantly to the organization and development of the GRA in general.

assionate about their sport, dedicated to the friendships they established, and committed to building an association which gave rodeo cowgirls fair and equitable opportunities to compete, the GRA's early leaders built a close-knit team. It is admirable, but not surprising, that the vast majority of the girls who were charter members of the GRA, or joined during the association's earliest days, continued to show up at virtually every event for the next five years.

They were part of the "sisterhood," and they knew the other girls were counting on their active participation to ensure the GRA's success. When packing up and leaving one rodeo the girls would build support for the next by calling to each other "be sure to show up in San Angelo"—or wherever the next event was scheduled—"so that we have enough contestants to put on a good show."

As a result, the GRA immediately experienced solid growth. The thirty-eight women from the initial February, 1948 San Angelo meeting had become seventy-four GRA charter members, participating in sixty sanctioned events by the end of that first year. In July of 1950 more than one hundred members represented eleven states and one Canadian province, due in no small part to James Cathey's role as GRA publicity director and his new GRA magazine, *Powder Puff and Spurs,* which had quickly grown to serve subscribers in thirty-one states and Canada.

The GRA expanded on many fronts. Sanctioned roping events spread across the West, sometimes offering sizable purses to the winners. In 1948, a jackpot calf roping at Claude, Texas, attracted a field of fourteen top ropers including Sawyer, Binford, Barton, Worthington and Montgomery. From then on through the mid-fifties, communities in Texas, New Mexico, Oklahoma, Colorado, Wyoming and Nebraska held events such as matched calf roping, jackpot calf roping, and team roping. Nineteen-year-old Ruby Gobble launched her professional career at the 1950 Pikes Peak or Bust Rodeo at Colorado Springs, where she won the cowgirl calf roping. Gobble also took the title at a highly publicized Northwest all-girl calf roping at Laramie, Wyoming, on July 11, 1952. Other top finishers there included Dixie Reger, Judy Hays, Wanda Harper, Blanche Altizer Smith and Margaret Owens Montgomery.[26]

Barrel racing grew exponentially, spreading especially as a GRA-sanctioned event in RCA rodeos. Sensing the direction, younger cowgirls concentrated on this area and often 50% or more of entries in the all-girl rodeos were barrel racers.

The sheer number of all-girl rodeos also grew, with twenty-four held in 1950 alone. Binford and Farr produced contests in Amarillo, San Angelo, and Seymour, Texas, as well as Colorado Springs, Colorado, and Natchez, Mississippi. However, the women did not maintain a monopoly on the business for long. Attracted by their success and the widespread support for women's rodeo in general, several men including Dub Spence and Jerry Rippeteau began producing "all-girl" shows, where the performers were female, but the remaining staff were male. Others such as Delbert Lyons and the Beutler Brothers specialized in providing rough stock appropriate to the women. Dan Coates honed his announcing skills for women's rodeo as did Nat Flemming, joining Monte Reger, who had announced the historic 1947 Tri-State All Girl Rodeo in Amarillo.

In October of 1949, Rippeteau introduced all-girl rodeo to Corpus Christi, Texas, producing the GRA Championship

---

26 LeCompte, 163.

event. Publicity was virtually nil that year, resulting in disappointing crowds, but the following year, he turned every crank possible, the newspaper covered it in style, and the fans embraced the cowgirls with open arms. Spence's May, 1950, contest at Coleman, Texas, was likewise a huge success. It overcame two days of torrential rains to draw not only enthusiastic crowds but the largest numbers ever for the women's sport.

Rippeteau also produced the GRA Championship Rodeo in October, 1950, at Tulsa's indoor fairgrounds pavilion and again in November, 1951.

The finals moved to the Fairgrounds in Dallas for 1953–55, where the contests drew sizable crowds and extensive press, although the publicity generated by the male producers rarely came close to the quality and quantity Nancy and Thena Mae elicited with the able assistance of GRA publicity director James Cathey.

Despite their excellent publicity and support, Nancy and Thena Mae's rodeo business had managed to break even but never showed a profit. Predictions that their all-girl rodeos would play Madison Square Garden were never realized, and they eventually dissolved Tri-State All Girl Rodeo Inc. in 1953. Despite the men's meager publicity efforts, quite a few were producing GRA contests, and Nancy and Thena Mae believed that all-girl rodeos were sufficiently established to succeed without their corporation.[27]

By 1953, the GRA was definitely an organization in transition. The composition of that tight-knit group of early cowgirls who traveled from rodeo to rodeo was changing, with its members heading in different directions. The deep-seated friendships remained, but some of the original leaders were settling into new roles. Nancy and Thena Mae had each completed a term as GRA president. With the closing of their production company, their participation in

27 Ibid., 164.

rodeos moved more to cutting horse competitions, and they each began to gravitate toward other pursuits related to ranch ownership and management. Fern Sawyer had essentially retired from competitive rodeo by 1951 to devote more time to her ranch and New Mexico politics. She only occasionally participated in cutting contests, or filled in as a heeler in team roping events, although she did continue to serve as a timer or judge at some GRA events. Margaret Owens Montgomery, having served two terms as GRA president (1948–49) and another couple of terms as a supporting board member, was still an active competitor at many GRA events, but she had stepped back from her former leadership role to allow some of the other girls to assume more responsibility. The GRA's first vice president, Dude Barton, had realized early on in 1948 that the demands of single handedly running her own ranch while maintaining a leadership role in the GRA were entirely too time consuming, so she asked the other girls to elect someone else to the board when her year as vice president was over. Dude continued to be an ardent supporter of the GRA and competed in events that were relatively close to her ranch on the North Pease river whenever she could, but her availability was limited, and she participated in her final GRA rodeo in Colorado Springs at the end of the 1953 season. After 1953, only occasionally did Ruby Gobble compete in a rodeo, working mostly on the Binford ranch, and likewise, rough stock specialist Rose Garrett was gone from the scene. Trick rider Mitzi Lucas Riley had married and by 1952 was a mother, stepping back from performing to devote most of her time to raising her young son. Another star going through changes was Dixie Reger, who served as the official GRA clown from 1948 until 1953. Once the organization was formed, Dixie devoted her entire career to women's rodeos, serving as both clown and contract performer. She also competed in many of the contests, enjoying her greatest success in calf roping. Her dedication helped the fledgling organization survive, and she served as GRA vice president from 1950 to 1952. After the last performance at the 1953 Colorado Springs Rodeo, some of the girls were sitting around having a drink and chatting when Dixie announced, "Well girls, that's it. I'm retiring from rodeo and getting married." And she did.

After James Cathey's year as Publicity Director concluded in 1951, he continued to ardently support the GRA, photographing their rodeos and other events. But his growing business was moving in new directions. Although he remained closely involved with many of the GRA founders throughout the remainder of his thirty-year photojournalism career, James discontinued publication of *Powder Puff and Spurs* by mid 1952 and directed his time and energy into other areas.

Jackie Worthington stepped up to the GRA presidency for three terms, beginning in 1954, and she recognized the need to cement the GRA's relationship with the RCA. On January 30, 1955, she and RCA president Bill Linderman signed the following historic agreement, still in effect today:

"Only Rodeo Cowboys' Association, Inc. cards will be honored by the Girls' Rodeo Association and the Rodeo Cowboys' Association, Inc. will strongly urge and recommend the use of G.R.A. girls in barrel racing in related events. In the case of straight rodeos, the Rodeo Cowboys' Association, Inc. will insist that such events conform to Rodeo Cowboys' Association, Inc. and G.R.A. rules and regulations. This agreement shall be in effect until such time as it is terminated by action of either of the parties hereto."[28]

This agreement brought the RCA and GRA closer together and set the stage for barrel racing to become the

---

28 Ibid., 162.

signature event that it is today. While desire for opportunities to compete in roping and rough stock events were key motivators leading to the original all-girl rodeos and the formation of the GRA, those events would eventually be supplanted by the preeminence of barrel racing.

The subtle evolution that had begun to affect the GRA sisterhood in 1953 was, at first, noticeable only in hindsight. However, by 1955, with the departure of many of the association's founding members and dynamic early leaders, it was becoming apparent that the GRA was nearing the end of an era and beginning to embark on a new direction. The line of demarcation between one era and the next would become abundantly clear on October 8, 1955, when the GRA's founding president and first World Champion Cowgirl, Margaret Owens Montgomery, died in a tragic automobile accident.

*T*his book focuses on telling the story of a few key individuals who played leading roles in the incubation, creation and development of the Girls Rodeo Association from the late 1940s through the early 1950s.

However, many exceptional women came to the association a little later on, making significant contributions at critical junctures. They led the association through challenging times and new developments, including the updating of the name to Women's Professional Rodeo Association (WPRA), to its current position as not only the oldest women's professional sports association in the United States but possibly its most dynamic.

The following is a small tip of the hat to four of those women. They each exhibit strikingly similar individual leadership skills: strength of character, steely determination, and the same plain old cowgirl grit that the GRA founders possessed in abundance.

James Cathey photo–2015.006.2.5.59.35

Billie Hinson McBride, February, 1959.

Billie Hinson McBride

Born in Copperas Cove, Texas, in 1927, Billie Hinson McBride fell in love with barrel racing when she first saw the event as a ten-year-old. She became a charter member of the Girls Rodeo Association in 1948 and served as director, secretary, vice president and president over a period of thirteen years.

In the 1950s, Billie's barrel racing skills were unparalleled. After picking up a Reserve World Championship in 1954, she went on the longest streak of the young association's history, winning four consecutive world championships from 1955 to 1958 on her great mare, Zombie. In doing so, she set a record which stood for three decades, not broken until Charmayne James won her fifth title in 1988.

As president, McBride spearheaded an effort to get the GRA barrel race included with the newly formed National Finals Rodeo (NFR) being produced by the Rodeo Cowboys Association. Though that original effort proved unsuccessful, she did secure a spot for the ladies with the National Finals Steer Roping, held in Clayton, NM, in 1959, an event that paved the way for the barrels to make the jump into the NFR a few years later.[29]

"It was bone chilling cold in Clayton that year," recalled Florence Youree in a 2018 interview, "and the wind was howling something awful." But the girls were happy to have the opportunity to compete even in this limited version of the National Finals, and grateful to Billie for helping to take them one step closer to full acceptance.

Billie was inducted into the Texas Rodeo Cowboy Hall of Fame and the National Cowgirl Hall of Fame in 1981, and she was inducted into the ProRodeo Hall of Fame in 2018.

Florence Youree

The eldest daughter of Lena and John Henry Price, Florence and her younger sister Sherry (Combs Johnson) grew up on the family ranch in Duncan, Oklahoma. Florence began her rodeo career at AJRA events in 1951 and started running barrels while attending Oklahoma State University, where she met her husband, Dale Youree.

Joining the GRA in 1953, Florence served as a director for seventeen years, holding the office of president from 1960 to 1964. She also continued as the association's secretary until the 1970s.

During Florence's tenure with the GRA she was constantly focused on getting more prize money for the group's events. "I really liked selling," she said. "If someone offered to put up an extra $100 in prize money, I'd say how about $150, and they would usually agree to it."

James Cathey photo–2015.006.2.5.59.14

Florence Youree, February, 1959.

29 Jolee Jordan and Ann Bleiker, "Pro Rodeo Hall of Fame Inductees Announced," *WPRA NEWS*, April 2018, 14–15.

In 1954, she met with the RCA board to sign an agreement for them to officially recognize the GRA and back their events with 10 percent of the prize money. And, in 1967, when the NFR first moved to Oklahoma City, Florence not only led the effort to have the GRA barrel race included in the NFR but also met with Stanley Draper, Jr. of the OKC Chamber of Commerce and convinced them to put up an additional $1,000 in prize money.

Although the GRA had been crowning national champions for years, getting the barrel race included in the NFR was a public relations coup. The GRA had finally gained acceptance at the highest levels of professional rodeo and barrel racing soon became one of rodeo's most popular events.

Florence was founder and president of Barrel Futurities of America, and she was the organizer of the Oklahoma Youth Rodeo Association. She and Dale founded the first riding school in the country, where they trained barrel horses and conducted riding clinics throughout the nation for more than ten years.

The Yourees are the first family to have three generations qualify for the NFR, Florence (eight times), her daughter Renee Ward, and her granddaughter Janae Ward, who was the World Champion Barrel Racer in 2003. Another grand-daughter, Kylie Weast, is on track to make the NFR in 2018 as this book goes to press.

Florence was the 1966 All-Around GRA World Champion and 1993 Coca Cola Woman of the Year. She was Inducted into the National Cowgirl Hall of Fame in 1996 and the Barrel Racing Pro Tour Hall of Fame in 2004.

Mildred Farris

"I always wanted to be in rodeo," said Mildred Farris upon her joint induction into the ProRodeo Hall of Fame along with her husband, John Farris, in 2006.

Mildred was born to Blanche and W.B. Cotten in

James Cathey photo–2015.006.10.6.7.97

Mildred Farris, October, 1957.

Andrews, Texas, on August 8, 1933. After graduating from Andrews High School, she attended Sul Ross College in Alpine, Texas, where she was a member of the rodeo team and earned a degree in physical education.

Mildred married John Farris, a fellow rodeo contestant, in 1955, and they embarked on a fifty-eight-year journey together that would take them to virtually every corner of the world of rodeo. An avid barrel racer, she joined the Texas Barrel Racers Association and won the championship three consecutive years, in 1955, 1956, and 1957.

Joining the GRA in 1958, Mildred continued her active participation in barrel racing, qualifying for the National Finals Rodeo thirteen times. She finished as Reserve World Champion in 1959, 1960, and 1969, and she posted the fastest time at the NFR in 1968.

During her tenure as GRA director of barrel racing, vice president, and president (1965–71), Mildred worked diligently to get barrel racing introduced at rodeos across the country. One of the innovations in barrel racing under her rule was the introduction of the five-second penalty for knocked over barrels, and she worked to help bring electronic eyes to pro barrel racing. She also noted that in those days the prizes for barrel racing were not comparable to the men's events. If the men's bronc riding or roping paid $400 to win, the barrel racing paid around $100 to the winner. She is quite proud to say that in today's rodeo the WPRA-sanctioned barrel racing events pay comparable monies to sanctioned events of the Professional Rodeo Cowboys Association (PRCA).[30]

Both John and Mildred retired from rodeo competition in the mid-1970s but continued to work in rodeos for many years, he as a stock handler and chute manager and she as a secretary, dedicating her time to the NFR, PRCA

---

30 Gail Woerner, "The History of Barrel Racing," *Way Out West Blog*, October 28, 2014. http://www.gailwoerner.com/way-out-west-blog/the-history-of-barrel-racing

and WPRA. In addition to John and Mildred being the first couple jointly inducted into the ProRodeo Hall of Fame in 2006, she was inducted into the Sul Ross Hall of Fame in 1994, selected WPRA Woman of The Year in 1996, named PRCA Secretary of the Year nine-times, and inducted into the Texas Rodeo Cowboy Hall of Fame in 2004, the National Cowboy & Western Heritage Museum's Rodeo Hall of Fame (along with John) in 2010 and the National Cowgirl Hall of Fame in 2012.

Jimmie Gibbs Munroe

Born into the heritage of the 101 Ranch, Jimmie Gibbs Munroe was the granddaughter of Colonel Zack Miller, co-founder of the legendary 101 Ranch Wild West Show. She began her rodeo career early and was a champion in junior and high school rodeos before entering Sam Houston State University, where she was a member of the 1974 national championship rodeo team.

At SHSU Jimmie earned three individual national titles, one for barrel racing, and all-around titles in two years, setting the stage for a professional career that included eleven trips to the NFR with three different horses and, in 1984, winning the most money of all the contestants. Munroe also holds five world titles within the Women's Professional Rodeo Association in the categories of barrel racing, tie-down roping, and all-around champion.

However, it's Jimmie's contributions outside the arena that make her one of the most important GRA/WPRA leaders of all time. She was elected president of the GRA in 1978 and served for an unprecedented fourteen straight years, leading the association through a name change to the Women's Professional Rodeo Association (WPRA) in 1981. She worked to obtain national sponsors and led the association in finally acquiring equal prize money to the men. Under Jimmie's

Photographer unknown, provided by Jimmie Munroe
Jimmie Gibbs Munroe, 1980.

In 1975 Jimmie Gibbs Munroe was the World Champion Barrel Racer and took home a record-setting $22,769 that year.

In 2018, while browsing through her old scrapbooks, Jimmie came upon a note from James Cathey and sent it to us to read. In it he said:

"Congratulations, Jimmie.

In the early 1950s, right after the GRA was formed and even before you were born, it was the dream of all those girls to see the day when a barrel racer could win into the five figures for a year. I know about their dreams and desires, because as publicity director for the GRA, it was my responsibility to build a springboard which would accomplish their goal.

Thank you for making this dream come true for all those girls who fought so hard to get barrel racing recognized and established as a main rodeo event.

May God Bless You.

James Cathey"

leadership, the WPRA instituted the mandatory use of electronic timers at barrel racing events and worked to produce better arena conditions throughout rodeo.

As if she hadn't already done enough, after an 18-year hiatus, Jimmie returned to serve two more years as WPRA President, from 2011–2012.

Jimmie was inducted into the National Cowgirl Hall of Fame in 1992, Texas Rodeo Cowboy Hall of Fame in 1997, Texas Cowboy Hall of Fame in 2003, and National Cowboy & Western Heritage Museum's Rodeo Hall of Fame in 2016. In 1990, she was named Coca-Cola Woman of the Year in Professional Rodeo, and in 1996 she received the Tad Lucas Award from the Rodeo Historical Society.

Yes, they were tough contenders in the rodeo arena, but they were also women of style. This iconic James Cathey photo is of six GRA leaders taking part in the GRA Fashion Show at the Western Hills Hotel in conjunction with the 1959 Fort Worth Southwestern Exposition Stock Show and Rodeo. From left to right: Sherry Combs Johnson, Billie McBride, Berva Dawn Taylor, Manuelita Mitchell-Woodward, Florence Youree and Wanda Kinkeade, champions and beauties, all.

lthough many of the talented women who formed the
GRA remained active and involved in the organization,
others moved on. They were proud to have provided a venue
for women to compete in rodeo, but in the mid-1950s, as
they grew older, had families, and the organization began to
stand on its own, they found other challenges and ventures
to pursue. The grit and determination that led to their
becoming world champions wasn't just something they
picked up to form an organization. Their determination and
thirst for adventure, novelty, and community were deep-seated character traits that helped them excel in their post-rodeo
lives as much or more than they had during the founding of
the GRA.

After Nancy Binford and Thena Mae Farr closed down
their rodeo production company at the end of 1953, both
women continued to compete in GRA events for some time,
but after 1953 they began to gravitate back to their roots as
ranch owners and managers.

Nancy Binford joined her mother, Katherine, in
managing the M Bar ranch in Wildorado, Texas, where she
had grown up. She ventured into Quarter Horse breeding
and for several years owned a couple of racing stables as well
as a western wear store in Amarillo. She helped organize
the American Quarter Horse Association and the National
Cutting Horse Association. Nancy also served on a number
of community boards and 4-H committees.

Thena Mae Farr returned to manage her family's ranch
in Seymour, Texas. In 1955, she was injured in a hunting-re-
lated accident which cut short her days as an active rodeo

competitor. She did, however, continue as a very active ranch manager, civic volunteer and 4-H Leader. Thena Mae was a member of the Texas and Southwestern Cattle Raisers Association, the American Cattle Raisers Association, the West Texas Chamber of Commerce, the Seymour Remuda Club, the Baylor County Farm Bureau, and the American Quarter Horse Association.

Margaret Owens Montgomery, the GRA's first president and winner of the 1948 All-Around championship, continued her participation in the association, serving in several different board positions and remaining an active rodeo competitor until her untimely death in an auto accident in 1955. Margaret will forever be remembered as one of the most competitive and athletically gifted GRA members of all time.

Dude Barton continues to live on the S-Bar ranch where she grew up. For many years she raised cattle and Quarter Horses and managed her farm, often spending up to ten hours a day on her tractor. Now, well into her nineties, Dude still does a little farming but mostly stays busy with woodworking. She makes footstools, bird houses and picture frames using the wood she salvaged from the floors of her family's old farm house, which she converted to a barn several years ago when she built her new home. Dude occasionally drives her car into the small towns near her ranch and seems to relish the fact that everyone she encounters calls her "Aunt Dude."

Jackie Worthington had always worked on the family's West Fork Creek Ranch and remained true to her roots. A fierce competitor who loved rodeo, she pursued her competitive goals as long as she possibly could. Upon retiring with twenty-three world championships to her credit, Jackie settled back at the ranch to help her father with management. Whether in the world of rodeo, ranching or civic endeavors, the stories are legion about what a wonderful, generous and truly helpful friend Jackie was to everyone she met.

Dixie Reger Mosley retired in 1953. After seventeen years as a rodeo performer, clown and contestant, she said, "It was time." When she married a few weeks after her retirement, Dixie had been a rodeo cowgirl so long that it only seemed natural to wear her boots under her wedding gown. But she poured herself 100 percent into a new life with her husband, William, and their children. After they married, Bill returned to college and Dixie jokes that she earned her PHT (Put Husband Through). She left rodeo behind and, true to her word, never rode a horse again. But she has maintained a very close and supportive relationship with other members of the GRA "sisterhood" throughout the past sixty-plus years, and she is a regular attendee at annual National Cowgirl Hall of Fame induction ceremonies.

Tad Lucas was well established and widely recognized as the "First Lady of Rodeo" by the time the GRA was founded in 1948. At age forty-five, her mere presence among the membership gave the association credibility and a stature it may not have otherwise enjoyed. So what did she do with her matriarchal role? She became a clown, because that's what the GRA needed at that time. That's the way Tad was—she loved rodeo in all its forms and was happy to fill whatever role she could: bronc rider, trick rider, secretary, timer, judge or clown. Tad continued to perform at rodeos until 1964 and then spent many years on the board of directors of the Rodeo Historical Society before passing away in 1990. The RHS now presents the annual Tad Lucas Award to the most outstanding female contributor to the sport of rodeo.

Fern Sawyer stayed active in rodeo judging and in managing her ranch. She was also active in New Mexico politics and served on the Board of the State Fair and the Racing Commission. For many years Fern was the standard bearer carrying the American flag at the opening of the All American Futurity at Ruidoso Downs and the New Mexico

State Fair in Albuquerque. Shortly after her death, at the opening of every performance of that year's Fair, a horse with an empty saddle was led around the arena as the audience stood in several minutes of deafening silence, honoring the state's most legendary cowgirl. Always known for her flamboyant style, Fern died at age seventy-six with her boots on—one of her 150 pair of custom-made, hand-tooled boots, most likely color-matched to her spandex riding pants. Fittingly, her tombstone reads "Lived Large," and indeed, she did.

Blanche Altizer Smith was born into a South Texas ranching family, and when not following the rodeo circuit, she spent her entire life in the area near Del Rio. The GRA's first secretary, Blanche was a champion calf roper, team roper, and barrel racer. Following her retirement from competition, she served as secretary and timer for numerous professional rodeos, junior rodeos, 4-H stock shows and roping events. Her husband, Bud, and their two children, Jim and Olie, were also involved in professional rodeo.

Wanda Harper Bush was just sixteen when she joined the GRA. As one of its youngest charter members, Wanda came into her own as a competitor in the early 1950s and went on to establish a career as the most decorated cowgirl in GRA/WPRA history, with thirty-two world titles. She served as a board member for twenty years, returning in the late 1980s to help then WPRA president Jimmie Munroe in her quest to secure equal money for WPRA contestants at PRCA rodeos. Wanda continued helping young people through 4-H and began offering barrel racing clinics helping scores of up-and-coming barrel race stars. She was widely known as the "best horsewoman ever" and was revered by her many students.

Betty Dusek, the GRA's first calf roping director, continued competing into her seventies, also managing the stock part of the ranch she shared with her husband while he managed the farm. Betty won her last saddle in competition at a West Texas Rodeo Association event in 2005 at age seventy-four. Late in her career Betty took special pride in beating all of the "young girls"—as she referred to any woman under age 50—who competed against her.

Rae Beach continued as an active competitor in GRA rodeos through 1963, the year she won her eighth and final bareback bronc riding world championship. Born in California, Rae became a resident of Texas in 1949, working as a cowgirl for the Farr Ranch in Seymour. She later moved to Fort Worth where she worked for Ryon's and Leddy's western stores for many years. During the 1960s and 1970s she bred and raced Quarter Horses. Rae passed away in 1991 at the age of 63. Although her nomination to the National Cowgirl Hall of Fame has been actively supported by many of her fellow GRA competitors, Rae Beach has yet to be inducted into any rodeo hall of fame.

Ruby Gobble traveled the GRA rodeo circuit from her debut at the 1950 Pikes Peak or Bust Rodeo in Colorado Springs, through the mid 1950s, winning three world titles in team roping and one in ribbon roping. Following her competitive career, Ruby continued to work with Kate and Nancy Binford on the Binford ranch until 1963, when she became foreman of the legendary Chase Ranch in Cimarron, New Mexico. For the next 50 years, Ruby, along with Chase Ranch owner, Gretchen Sammis, used her versatile talents to keep the historic Hereford ranch running smoothly. Ruby was smart, hardworking, loyal, laughing, loving, and a lot of fun. Known for much more than her horsemanship, Ruby always attracted people to lively stories and her warm friendship.

The successor to the GRA, the WPRA, continues to flourish today, with its headquarters in Colorado Springs, Colorado, and members spread throughout the international rodeo community.

Widely known as the premier rodeo photojournalist of the "Golden Age" of rodeo, James Cathey was directly involved in the organization, promotion and growth of several levels of American rodeo. He worked with top RCA rodeos and tirelessly supported the National Intercollegiate Rodeo Association. As director of publicity for the GRA and the National High School Rodeo Association, he helped launch both organizations from regional to now international in scope.

A prolific rodeo journalist, Cathey served as editor and publisher of *Powder Puff & Spurs,* the monthly magazine of the GRA, and was the associate editor for rodeo at *Back in the Saddle* magazine and a contributing editor of rodeo articles and news for *Western Horseman, Hoofs & Horns,* and *American Quarter Horse Journal.* He was also a significant supplier of photographic images and news articles supporting the National Cutting Horse Association, Texas and Southwestern Cattle Raisers Association, and American Quarter Horse Association.

Attempting to shoot every contestant in every go-round, Cathey compiled a massive photographic record of the sport of American rodeo during the 1940s, 50s and 60s.

Cathey's most prized possession was a gold and sterling rodeo trophy buckle awarded to him in 1951 by the Josey's Ranch Rodeo in Carrollton, Texas. Rodeo producers have not been known for making such special awards to their contractors, but James Cathey was considered someone special to the rodeo.

Photo by the Authors—buckel from the Cathey family's collection

Beyond the rodeo arena—working horse shows and cow cutting events—Cathey began to specialize in photographing the champions of the working cow horse breed, the American Quarter Horse. For many years, he traveled across the western United States and Canada photographing Quarter Horses at home on their ranches, competing in cutting contests and winning halter and conformation classes at horse shows. Cathey was the very first professional to specialize in Quarter Horse photography, and he created the art and standards for portraiture of AQHA champions and bloodline sires.

Writing for *Hoofs & Horns* magazine in the mid 1960s, Marjorie Grant Burns said, "A lot of things have gone into the business of presenting the American Quarter Horse to the world, the most important of which is the photography of James Cathey of Fort Worth. Working constantly with camera and typewriter, he has done the job of a true craftsman, presenting pictures of near perfect quality and concept, strengthened by knowledge that can only be gained through years of tireless effort."

The more than 68,000 historic photographic negatives that comprise the James Cathey Heritage Collection have been professionally appraised, valued as unique 20th century artifacts, and declared a "National Treasure." As would surely have pleased the photographer, the entire collection from his life's work was donated to the American people and now resides at the Donald C. & Elizabeth M. Dickinson Research Center at the National Cowboy & Western Heritage Museum in Oklahoma City.

Cathey died on June 2, 1978 at age 61. He was inducted into the National Cowboy & Western Heritage Museum's Rodeo Hall of Fame in 2018.

James Cathey holding his first rodeo camera, a Graflex Speed Graphic, and standing in front of one of his photo displays, believed to have been photographed in Vernon, Texas, in May, 1951.

James Cathey photo–2015.006.11.11.1.8

WORLD CHAMPION COWGIRLS, 1951: (left to right) Lucyle Cowey, saddle bronc; Rae Beach, bareback; Ruby Gobble, team tying; Rose Garrett Brown, bull riding; Jackie Worthington, all-around and cutting horse; Wanda Harper Bush, calf roping and ribbon roping; Margaret Owens Montgomery, barrel racing; Sally Taylor, sportsmanship.

APPENDIX

GRA Founding Members

February 28, 1948
St. Angelus Hotel, San Angelo TX

Mrs. Russell Allen
Sissy Allen
Mrs. Curtis Barron
Dude Barton
Nancy Binford
Sug Owens Bloxom
Nancy Bragg
Iris Dorsett
Betty Barron Dusek
Thena Mae Farr
Frances Gist
Bebe Green
Helen Barron Green
Mary Green
Sally Hardin
Marlene Harlan
Fay Ann Horton
Tad Lucas
Manuelita Mitchell
Jesse Myers
Margaret Owens Montgomery
Mrs. Katherine Pearson
Mrs. Ted Powers
June Probst
Virginia Probst
Ora Altizer Quigg
Doris Reed
Dixie Reger
Mitzi Lucas Riley
Mary Ellen Sellers
Blanche Altizer Smith
Sally Taylor
Frances Weeg
Vivian White
Josephine Willis
Jackie Worthington
Ann Young
Izora Young

GRA Presidents (past)

!948 – 49	Margaret Owens Montgomery
1950	Nancy Binford
1951	Thena Mae Farr
1952 – 53	Billye Burk Gamblin
1954 – 56	Jackie Worthington
1957 – 59	Billie McBride
1960 – 64	Florence Youree
1965 – 71	Mildred Farris
1972 – 74	Margaret Clemons
1975	Sammie Fancher Thurman
1976 – 77	Kay Vamvoras
1978 – 93	Jimmie Gibbs Munroe*

*GRA name changed to Women's Professional
Rodeo Association (WPRA) in 1981

GRA Champions 1948–1970

1948
All-Around .... Margaret Owens
Bareback Riding.......... Jackie Worthington
Bull Riding .... Jackie Worthington
Calf Roping................. Betty Dusek
Team Roping.............. Blanche Smith
Barrel Race................. Margaret Owens
Cutting Horse .... Margaret Owens
Ribbon Roping .... Judy Hays

1949
All-Around .... Amy McGilvray
Bareback Riding.......... Jackie Worthington
Bull Riding .... Jackie Worthington
Calf Roping................. Betty Dusek
Team Roping.............. Margaret Owens
Barrel Race................. Amy McGilvray
Saddle Bronc .... Vivian White

1950
All-Around .... Jackie Worthington
Bareback Riding.......... Jackie Worthington
Bull Riding .... Jackie Worthington
CalfRoping.................. Blanche Smith
Team Roping.............. Blanche Smith
Barrel Race................. Latonne Sewalt
Cutting Horse .... Nancy Binford
Ribbon Roping .... Jackie Worthington

1951
All-Around .... Jackie Worthington
Bareback Riding.......... Rae Beach
Bull Riding .... Rose Garrett
Calf Roping................. Wanda Harper Bush
Barrel Race................. Margaret Owens
Ribbon Roping .... Wanda Harper Bush
Saddle Bronc .... Lucyle Cowey

1952
All-Around .... Wanda Harper Bush
Bareback Riding.......... Rae Beach
Bull Riding .... Tommie Green
Calf Roping................. Wanda Harper Bush
Team Tying .... Judy Hays
Barrel Race................. Wanda Harper Bush
Cutting Horse .... Jackie Worthington
Ribbon Roping .... Ruby Gobble

1953
All-Around .... Jackie Worthington
Bareback Riding .... Rae Beach
Bull Riding .... Jackie Worthington
Calf Roping................. Wanda Harper Bush

Team Tying .... Ruby Gobble
Barrel Race................. Wanda Harper Bush
Cutting Horse .... Jackie Worthington
Ribbon Roping .... Wanda Harper Bush

1954
All-Around .... Jackie Worthington
Bareback Riding.......... Rae Beach
Bull Riding .... Jackie Worthington
Calf Roping................. Wanda Harper Bush
Team Tying .... Betty Dusek
Barrel Race................. Latonne Sewalt
Cutting Horse .... Nancy Bragg
Ribbon Roping .... Wanda Harper Bush

1955
All-Around .... Jackie Worthington
Bareback Riding.......... Rae Beach
Bull Riding .... Jackie Worthington
Calf Roping................. Wanda Harper Bush
Team Tying .... Blanch Smith
Barrel Race................. Billie McBride
Cutting Horse .... Nancy Bragg

1956
All-Around .... Jackie Worthington
Bareback Riding.......... Rae Beach
Bull Riding .... Jackie Worthington
Calf Roping................. Wanda Harper Bush
Barrel Race................. Billie McBride
Cutting Horse .... Jackie Worthington
Ribbon Roping .... Wanda Harper Bush

1957
All-Around .... Wanda Harper Bush
Bareback Riding.......... Charlene Atkinson
Bull Riding .... Meta Adams
Calf Roping................. Fay Ann Horton Leach
Team Tying .... Jane Mayo
Barrel Race................. Billie McBride
Cutting Horse .... Jackie Worthington
Ribbon Roping .... Wanda Harper Bush

1958
All-Around .... Wanda Harper Bush
Bareback Riding.......... Charlene Atkinson
Bull Riding .... Meta Adams
Calf Roping................. Betty Dusek
Team Tying .... Jane Mayo
Barrel Race................. Billie McBride
Cutting Horse .... Jackie Worthington
Ribbon Roping .... Wanda Harper Bush

1959
All-Around .... Jane Mayo
Bareback Riding .... Charlene Atkinson
Bull Riding .... Meta Adams
Calf Roping .... Fay Ann Horton Leach
Team Tying .... Jane Mayo
Barrel Race .... Jane Mayo
Cutting Horse .... Jackie Worthington
Ribbon Roping .... Wanda Harper Bush

1960
All-Around .... Faye Ann Horton Leach
Barrel Race .... Jane Mayo
Calf Roping .... Wanda Harper Bush
(Incomplete Records)

1961
All-Around .... Sherry Combs Johnson
Bareback Riding .... Rae Beach
Calf Roping .... Betty Dusek
Barrel Race .... Jane Mayo
Cutting Horse .... Betty Ray

1962
All-Around .... Wanda Harper Bush
Calf Roping .... Wanda Harper Bush
Barrel Race .... Sherry Combs Johnson
(Incomplete records)

1963
All-Around .... Wanda Harper Bush
Bareback Riding .... Rae Beach
Bull Riding .... Bill Gay
Barrel Race .... Loretta Manuel
Cutting Horse .... Becky Ray
Flag Race .... Betty Dusek

1964
All-Around .... Wanda Harper Bush
Bareback Riding .... Jeanette Austin
Bull Riding .... Kathrine Theriot
Calf Roping .... Wanda Harper Bush
Barrel Race .... Ardith Bruce
Flag Race .... Fay Ann Horton Leach

1965
All-Around .... Wanda Harper Bush
Bull Riding .... Katherine Theriot
Calf Roping .... Rosalyn Mitchell
Barrel Race .... Sammie Thurman Brackenbury
Flag Race .... Betty Dusek
Ribbon Roping .... Rosalyn Mitchell

1966
All-Around .... Florence Youree
Bareback Riding .... Gloria Strickland
Calf Roping .... Wanda Harper Bush
Bull Riding .... Fay Ann Horton Leach
Barrel Race .... Norita Henderson
Cutting Horse .... Wanda Harper Bush
Flag Race .... Betty Dusek

1967
All-Around .... Betty Dusek
Bareback Riding .... Sandy McFarland
Bull Riding .... Sharon McFarland
Calf Roping .... Wanda Harper Bush
Barrel Race .... Loretta Manual
Cutting Horse .... Sandy Powell
Flag Race .... Betty Dusek
Ribbon Roping .... Betty Dusek

1968
All-Around .... Wanda Harper Bush
Bareback Riding .... Sandy Brewer
Bull Riding .... Sharon McFarland
Calf Roping .... Betty Dusek
Barrel Race .... Ann Lewis
Cutting Horse .... Sandy Powell
Flag Race .... Joyce Burk Loomis
Ribbon Roping .... Joyce Burk Loomis

1969
All-Around .... Wanda Harper Bush
Bareback Riding .... Kerry Grimes
Bull Riding .... Kerry Grimes
Calf Roping .... Betty Dusek
Barrel Race .... Missy Long
Cutting Horse .... Wanda Harper Bush
Flag Race .... Wanda Harper Bush
Ribbon Roping .... Terry Lewis

1970
All-Around .... Bonnie McPherson
Bareback Riding .... Bonnie McPherson
Bull Riding .... Bonnie McPherson
Calf Roping .... Betty Dusek
Barrel Race .... Joyce Burk Loomis
Cutting Horse .... Sandy Powell
Flag Race .... Betty Dusek
Pole Bending .... Bonnie McPherson
Steer Undecorating ..... Annette Duncan
Ribbon Roping .... Annette Duncan

SELECTED BIBLIOGRAPHY

This partial list from numerous articles, newspapers, archives, magazines, books, videos and films consulted, only begins to scratch the surface of the research behind this book. Hometown newspapers of the individual cowgirls were invaluable resources, often covering their exploits, triumphs and awards in great detail. Of special help were the comprehensive writings of Mary Lou LeCompte and Renée Laegreid and the phone calls and personal interviews with Dude Barton, Betty Dusek, Dixie Reger Mosley, Jimmie Gibbs Munroe, Rhonda Sedgwick-Stearns and Florence Youree.

Magazines:

Back in the Saddle
The Billboard
The Cattleman
GRA News
Hoofs and Horns
The Ketchpen
Powder Puff and Spurs
Quarter Horse Journal
Rodeo News
Texas Monthly
Western Horseman
WPRA NEWS

Newspaper Collections:

Newspapers.com.

Texas Tech University
Southwest Collection/Special Collections Library
https://swco-ir.tdl.org.

Blogs:

Harrison, Sally. *Sally Harrison's Blog.* www.sallyharrison.com.

Woerner, Gail Hughbanks, *Way Out West Blog,* http://www.gailwoerner.com/way-out-west-blog.

Archives, Museums and Associations:

National Cowboy & Western Heritage Museum, Dickinson Research Center, Oklahoma City, OK.

National Cowgirl Museum and Hall of Fame, Fort Worth, TX.

Professional Rodeo Association, Colorado Springs, CO.

Films:

Just for the Ride. (1996). [DVD] Directed by Amanda Micheli. New Mexico, Montana, Oklahoma: Runaway Films.

From Cheyenne to Pendleton: The Rise and Fall of the Rodeo Cowgirl. (2010). [DVD] Directed by Steve Wursta. Bend, OR: Arctic Circle Productions.

Books:

Burbick, Joan. *Rodeo Queens and the American Dream.* New York: Public Affairs, 2002.

Flood, Elizabeth Clair. *Cowgirls: Women of the Wild West.* Santa Fe, N.M.: Zon International Publishing, 2000.

Goldthwaite, Carmen. *Texas Ranch Women: Three Centuries of Mettle and Moxie.* Stroud, Gloucestershire: The History Press, 2014.

Jordan, Teresa. *Cowgirls: Women of the American West, An Oral History.* Garden City, NY: Anchor Press, 1982.

Kimball, Richard Ian. *Legends Never Die: Athletes and Their Afterlives in Modern America.* Syracuse: Syracuse University Press, 2017.

Lagreid, Renée M. "Ranch Women and Rodeo Performers in Post-World War II West Texas." In *Texas Women: Their Histories, Their Lives,* ed. Elizabeth Hayes Turner, Stephanie Cole, and Rebecca Sharpless. Athens, GA: University of Georgia Press, 2015.

Laegreid, Renée M. *Riding Pretty: Rodeo Royalty in the American West.* Lincoln, University of Nebraska Press, 2006.

LeCompte, Mary Lou. *Cowgirls of the Rodeo: Pioneer Professional Athletes.* Urbana: U of Illinois Press, 1993.

Patton, Tracey Owens, and Sally M. Shedlock. *Gender, Whiteness, and Power in Rodeo: Breaking Away from the Ties of Sexism.* Lanham, MD: Lexington Books, 2012.

Riske, Milt. *Those Magnificent Cowgirls: A History of the Rodeo Cowgirl.* Cheyenne: Wyoming Publishing, 1983.

Roach, Joyce Gibson. *The Cowgirls.* Denton: University of North Texas Press, 1977.

Thomas, Heidi M. *Cowgirls Up!: A History of Rodeo Women.* Guilford, CT: Twodot, 2014.

Wills, Kathy Lynn, and Virginia Artho. *Cowgirl Legends: From the Cowgirl Hall of Fame.* Salt Lake City: Gibbs Smith, 1994.

Wooden, Wayne S., and Cavin Ehringer. *Rodeo in America: Wranglers, Roughstock, and Paydirt.* Lawrence: University Press of Kansas, 1996.

Articles:

Brown, John. "Coming into their Own," *American Cowboy,* January/February 1997, 56-58.

Cathey, James. "The Girls Rodeo Association," *Back in the Saddle,* June 1950, 5.

Hirschfeld, Cindy. "Ride Like a Girl," *American Cowboy,* Nov. 2, 2012.

Jones, Kathryn. "Into the Sunset," *Texas Monthly,* February, 2003.

Lagreid, Renée M. "The Return of the Cowgirl Queen 'Performers Prove Beauty and Rodeo Can be Mixed,'" *Montana The Magazine of Western History,* Spring 2004, 44-55.

Lambert, Laura. 'Where are They Now? The History Behind the Jumping Cowgirl The Life of Dixie Reger," *WPRA NEWS,* June 2017, 46-47.

Lambert, Laura. "Where Are They Now? Betty Dusek-Paving the Way," *WPRA NEWS,* May 2017, 46.

Master, Rachael Stowe. "Riding Tall - and sideways, upside down, off the back of the horse..." *The TCU Magazine,* Fall 2002.

Owens, Margaret, *Girls Rodeo Magazine,* 1977, 12.

Owens, Sug,"Girls' Rodeo Association," *Hoofs and Horns,* May 1948.

Pattie, Jane. "Rodeo's First Lady, Tad Lucas," *The Quarter Horse Journal,* June 1961.

Porter, Willard. "Tad." *True West,* Sept. 1988.

---"Wanda's Some Cowgirl..." *Hoofs and Horns,* Aug. 1953.

Smith, Blanche Altizer. "The Girls Rodeo Association," *Western Horseman,* July 1953, 12.

Taylor, Lonn. "The Cowgirl Way," *Texas Monthly,* September 2015.

Toy, Chelsea. "History of the Rodeo Cowgirl," *American Cowboy,* August 3, 2012.

Walker, Charlene. "Not for Men Only," *Texas Techsan Magazine,* July/August 1972.

Woerner, Gail Hughbanks, "The History of Barrel Racing," *The Wrangler Network,* October 14, 2014. http://wranglernetwork.com/news/the-history-of-barrel-racing/.

Web Sites:

Oklahoma Historical Society, http://www.okhistory.org/index.php?fgn--search.

Texas Rodeo Cowboy Hall of Fame, https://www.texasrodeocowboy.com/story.html.

Texas Rodeo Hall of Fame, www.texasrodeohalloffame.com/.

Texas State Historical Association, https://www.tshaonline.org/home/.

The Portal to Texas History, https://texashistory.unt.edu/.

You Tube Videos:

Morris, Shirley. "Horrific Cowgirl Saddle Bronc Wreck 1929 Bonnie McCarroll," YouTube Video, August 9, 2011, https://www.youtube.com/watch?v=qtw-t7nvB8g.

INDEX OF INDIVIDUALS

Bold indicates found in the text. *Italics* indicate found in a photo caption.

Bold indicates found in the text. *Italics* indicate found in a photo caption.

CPSIA information can be obtained
at www.ICGtesting.com
Printed in the USA
LVHW052027091118
595686LV00001B/1/P